MW01293776

REVIEWS:

1) In *Ever Vigilant, Tales of the Vietnam War,* Specialist-4 Michael Hebert has written a compelling view of his tour of Vietnam, from his draft to his return Stateside. Done in vignette format, this exceptionally talented non-fiction writer covers his multifaceted experience with a rare honesty and self-effacing humor that makes reading his stories a joy.

Although the rest of the book absolutely covers the traumas of life in Vietnam, it does so in Hebert's charming style. Never grotesque, always respectful and entertaining (though be forewarned, it does use some of the racial terminology of the time in dialogue and thought segments).

The book is not <u>Platoon</u> or <u>Full Metal Jacket</u>; neither is it <u>Good Morning, Vietnam</u>. It neither pretends nor needs to be. Hebert brings his own experience as a Patrol Boat Specialist to the field, with his own voice, and that is more than sufficient. I heartily recommend this book to anyone interested in Vietnam history—or who simply enjoys a good story well-told.

Julia C. Hoover, MD, EdM
Reedsy Reviewer

2) In *Ever Vigilant: Tales of the Vietnam War*, author Michael J. Hebert chronicles his experiences as a young soldier. Like many young men of the time, Hebert finds camaraderie in his fellow soldiers, and the experiences of his time in Vietnam are forever etched in his memory. In this memoir, readers are invited into the daily lives of these soldiers, from the combat river patrols to the youthful downtime activities and everything in between.

I chose this book because I am both Vietnamese and a veteran and felt I would most likely relate to the cultural and military components of this story. Sure enough, I was pleasantly surprised! I found this to be refreshingly realistic and profound at the same time. The culture of Vietnam, as well as the sentiments of war, are captured here, not only by what is said but also by what is left unsaid.

The best part of the book is the vivid imagery and introspect used in the descriptions. I found that the author had some pretty astute observations. One of my favorite ones is when Hebert describes the traffic congestion in Saigon as a "choreographed dance of sorts." Another description that resonated with me was when he described locking eyes with an elderly woman in a field, and at that moment, he "came to appreciate the hardships of war and its effects on the Vietnamese people." A surprising touch of youthful humor punctuates the writing. The character development is also commendable.

I would not hesitate to give it a perfect rating because of the thoughtful descriptions and exceptional character development.

Kansas City Teacher/Online Book Club

PROLOGUE

War is carried out by young people trained for the task. It occurs at the edge of, or just over the edge, of what passes for civilized behavior.

Mike Hebert takes the reader along for his ride through his year in Vietnam. Hebert pays his dues and quickly learns how to handle his fast, heavily-armed PBR (patrol boat, river). He lands at a small outpost far up the coast; Vung Ro Bay. The Vung Ro detachment is small and remote. The order, organization, and discipline of regular units doesn't fit this tropical place of white sand beaches and turquoise water.

Vung Ro's idyllic setting is not without peril. Snipers, mortar barrages, and full-out perimeter assaults cut into the usual boredom of routine patrolling. Hebert's boat becomes a casualty of a rocket-propelled grenade.

The deadliest force he faces is not military—it is Mother Nature. Hebert and his crew ride out the fury of a typhoon as it lays waste to the small base. The account is harrowing as they seek safety in a storm that causes the end of the Vung Ro operation.

-Tom Wonsiewicz, Former XO, 458th TC, Vietnam

Ever Vigilant

Tales of the Vietnam War

Michael J. Hebert

Michael J. Hebert

Ever Vigilant, Tales of the Vietnam War

Copyright ©2022 by Michael J. Hebert
www.michaelhebert@cox.net

Library of Congress Control Number: 2021921783

All rights reserved. No part of this book may be reproduced or transmitted in any form or by any means without written permission from the author.

ISBN: 978-1-9818126-4-6 (Paperback)
ISBN: 978-8-7942920-8-4 (Hardback)
ISBN: 978-1-7352654-1-4 (E-book)

Printed in USA

FORWARD

During the Vietnam War, the United States Military employed heavily-armed high-speed gunboats to intercept and disrupt enemy travel on the rivers, bays, and deltas of South Vietnam. They were called PBR's, or River Patrol Boats. While the US Navy operated over 250 of these specialized watercraft, the US Army had less than 40.

The 458th Sea Tigers, an elite unit and the only one in the entire United States Army, operated River Patrol Boats in Vietnam. Headquartered in Saigon, the 458th PBR's had nine outposts scattered throughout South Vietnam: Cat Lo, Di An, Newport, Qui Nhon, Vung Ro Bay, Cam Ranh, Vung Tau, Cat Lai, and Cogido.

This book is based upon actual events that occurred in Vung Ro Bay, South Vietnam, from 1969 to 1970. While characters are based upon actual service members, some of the features and traits of persons depicted have been changed. Names have also been changed to protect the guilty!

US Army River Patrol Boat (PBR)

ACKNOWLEDGMENTS

Thanks to Tom Wonsiewicz, former 458th Executive Officer, for reading draft copies and offering advice, insightful script changes, and allowing me to use several of his photographs.

Thanks to my wife, Virginia, who found the time and patience to proofread and offer constructive re-writes and additions to this manuscript.

A heartfelt thank you to my dear cousin-in-law, Sallie Rhodes, and sister-in-law Marilyn Gayle, for having the time and patience to pre-edit my mess!

Thanks to Chas Rynberg and Tom Farrell for allowing me to use several photos and some of their memories.

A very special thank you goes out to Lou Baumann, who, thankfully, remembers almost everything that occurred during our year in Vietnam. Without his incredible recall, most of this book could not have been written. Lou also graciously contributed many of the story ideas.

Thank you also to Chris Schuehle for allowing me to use the true memoir of his horrific ordeal in Vung Ro, June 1968. (Chapter 11).

My appreciation to former Vietnam helicopter pilot Lt. David Parsley for allowing me to use several of his photos of the Vietnamese people and Saigon street scenes.

I owe a debt of gratitude to my dear sister, Susan Pearson, for her sharp-eyed proofreading of the finished script.

And last but certainly not least, I need to offer my sincere thanks and appreciation to my outstanding editor, Michael Sanders (Reedsy.com), for taking the time and effort to go through my manuscript with a fine-tooth comb and make much-needed suggestions and re-writes where it was needed.

For further information on the 458th Sea Tigers, please visit:

www.SeaTigersofVungRoBay.com
www.458thSeaTigers.org

For more book selections about River Patrol operations and the Vietnam War, please visit:

www.gunboatpress.com

DEDICATION

This book is dedicated to the brave soldiers, sailors, marines, and airmen who fought and died for their country, not only in Vung Ro Bay but throughout Vietnam.

"Tweeter was a Boy Scout—'course he went to Vietnam...
And found out the hard way, nobody gives a damn."

Tatum and the Monkey Man
The Traveling Wilburys

"A man can fight if he can see daylight
down the road somewhere.
But there ain't no daylight in Vietnam.
There's not a bit."

Lyndon B. Johnson

"How long do you Americans want to fight?
One year? Two years? Three years?
Five years? Ten years? Twenty years?
We will be glad to accommodate you."

Pham Von Dong
North Vietnamese Prime Minister
December 1966

CONTENTS

18th MP Brigade Patch

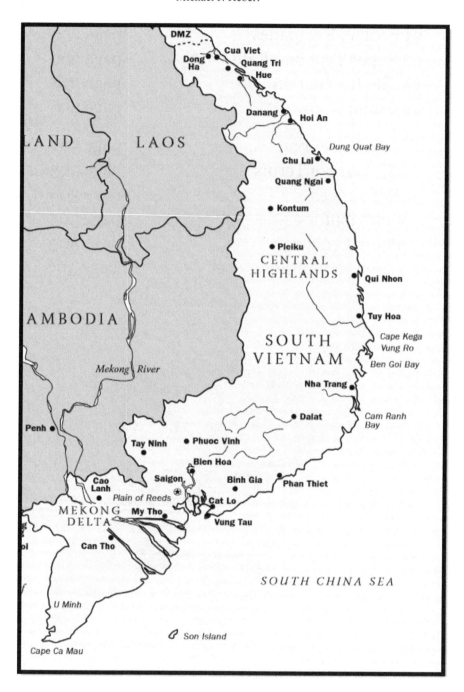

Map of Vietnam (Naval History & Heritage Command)

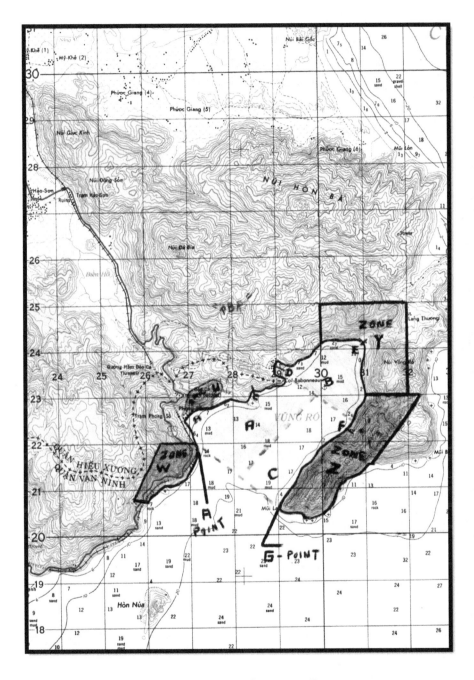

Map of Vung Ro Bay, PBR patrol areas, fire support zones

1. Operation Market Time

Late in the morning on February 16, 1965, a UH-1B medevac helicopter piloted by 1st Lieutenant James S. Bowers lifted off the pad at Qui Nhon on the central coast of South Vietnam and headed south. He flew along the mountains with steep slopes covered in dark green carpets of jungle foliage. Approaching a small cove called Vung Ro Bay, he surveyed the pristine sapphire waters of the bay below. Focusing on a small vegetation-covered island, he suddenly realized that it was slowly moving.

North Vietnamese Trawler

Swooping down for a closer look, he saw that the "island" was actually a trawler whose decks and superstructure had been camouflaged with potted plants and trees. Little wooden sampans were busy shuttling cargo between the ship and shore. Stacked in piles along the beach were cases and cases of wood crates filled with weapons and ammunition.

Lt. Bowers immediately radioed the find to LCDR Harvey P. Rodgers, the Senior Advisor to the South Vietnamese Navy's 2nd Coastal District, headquartered in Nha Trang, 95 kilometers to the south. LCDR Rodgers notified District Commander Ho Van Ky Thoai, who dispatched two South Vietnamese A-1 Skyraiders to the bay, where they capsized and sank the ship. Additional airstrikes the following day destroyed most of the stores onshore.

Weapons Cache in Vung Ro Bay

On February 19[th,] the South Vietnamese escort *Chi Lang II,* the medium landing ship *Tien Giang,* and the submarine chaser *Tuy Dong* arrived with soldiers, naval commandos, and US Navy Advisor Lt. Franklin W. Anderson.

Overcoming enemy small arms fire, the group discovered the wrecked ship and scores of weapons strewn about the beach. They recovered 100 tons of Soviet and Chinese-made war material, including close to 4,000 rifles and machine guns, 1 million rounds of small arms ammunition, 1,500 hand grenades, 2,000 mortar rounds, and 500 pounds of explosives.

For many years American analysts had doubted that the Communists were using the sea to supply their forces in the South, but the Vung Ro Incident proved them wrong. This led to the creation of the US Navy's Operation Market Time, a program initiated by General William Westmoreland to blockade the South Vietnamese coast and prevent communist ships from re-supplying North Vietnamese and Viet Cong troops.

The blockade continued for 8½ years and proved to be very successful.

2. Going to Vietnam

Raising the heavy sledgehammer-like bead breaker high above my head, I swung with all my might at the tractor-trailer rim lying on the floor of the Maintenance Shop. The objective was to hit a narrow channel between the rubber of the tire and the steel rim of the wheel, breaking the bond and allowing the tire to be removed.

Whang! It rang out.

"Damn," I winced. I missed and hit the rim of the wheel. The painful vibration traveled up my arms as I made another attempt, this time with success. Successive strikes, some successful, some not, for the better part of the next twenty minutes, left me in agony.

But the tire was off the rim.

I was not fond of changing the massive split-rim tires on the big rigs. At eighteen, I had minimal sledgehammer-swinging experience. I was lucky, though, in that there was another employee who usually changed the tires. On this night, however, he had called in sick. After much caution, I completed the task, placed the massive tire in a protective cage, and inflated it. My supervisor had warned me with numerous horror stories of people in other truck stops trying to inflate the wheels on the floor and the split rim blowing off and severely injuring or even killing them.

I was determined not to allow that to happen to me.

The night shift at the Big Wheel Truck Stop in Millersville, MD, was an adventure every night. I loved the smell of the truck stop: diesel fuel and hot rubber. Some nights I would stand in the middle of the fuel bays just inhaling: *diesel, diesel, diesel.* The pungent smell was overpowering.

The bosses were gone at night, and things were mostly quiet. I had a crush on Linda Dunn, the girl working the restaurant counter. She had soft white skin, hazel blue eyes, and light brown hair that cascaded over her shoulders. I kept badgering her for a date. She had just recently turned twenty.

"I can't go out with you," she said. "I'm older than you are."

"Oh yeah, you're only eighteen months older," I replied.

"Yeah, but you're in your teens. I'm in my twenties! That's a huge difference."

"Besides," she firmly reminded me one morning, "I'm management."

Nonetheless, we enjoyed each other's company and frequently engaged in harmless flirting.

We both got off work at 9:00 am. Being a bit of a prankster, one of my favorite lines was going up to her at quitting time and asking, "Hey Linda, are you Dunn?"

I thought my wit was hilarious.

She would just glare at me. "God, you're dumb."

·

My job was to fuel up the big rigs when they came in off Highway 301, just south of Glen Burnie, Maryland. The driver would pull up to a pump, shut the truck down, then go into the restaurant for a meal and perhaps a shower while I filled the massive tanks on either side of the cab. It usually took fifteen to twenty minutes to service a rig. While the tanks were fueling, I would climb up on the front bumper and give the windshield a thorough cleaning.

I got good tips.

The truck stop had a vast unpaved parking lot. It was customary for the pump boys to move the rigs out to the lot after refueling, so the drivers didn't have to interrupt their meals just to come out and park their truck.

That was the part of the job that I loved the most. Hop into the cab, fire up the giant diesel engine, depress the clutch and gently slip the truck into gear. It was unfortunate that I never got the chance to experiment with the transmissions, though. By the time I got up enough speed to change a gear, I was already at the parking area. Still, it was an incredible thrill for a teenager. It seemed to me like an exciting life, so much so that I had pretty much decided that I would like to be an over-the-road truck driver one day.

The sun came up before my shift was over. Day after day, I would watch the big rigs depart the parking area, screaming and whistling down the highway, smoke billowing from the colossal twin smokestacks rising behind the cabs. The sun's early morning rays would catch the smoke making little white curls as it spewed from the pipes. It never failed to fascinate me.

The only downside to my job was the diesel odor. As a young man, I loved every minute of it. The sweet, pungent smell of fresh diesel stayed in my nostrils for hours after I left work. Unfortunately, it also lingered on me. No matter how long I stayed in the shower, no matter how hard I scrubbed with soap, the smell of diesel was always a part of me. Smelling like diesel, however, was somehow—in my mind—a rite of passage. It was a manly odor, not for kids.

I often wondered if people talked about me behind my back, though: *Oh, there goes that diesel-stink kid. He's a nice enough young man, but my God, he smells like a Mack truck!*

I had only been working at the truck stop for the summer, which was quickly coming to an end. I studied automotive engineering at a school in Fayetteville, North Carolina, and returned home to keep my mother and two sisters' company until the fall. My father, a career Army sergeant, had been sent to Thailand a couple of months earlier for a one-year assignment.

.

I was walking up the sidewalk to my house after retrieving the day's mail, flipping through the envelopes, when I spotted it. My heart sank. It was what I had feared for quite some time.

My mother noticed the look on my face as soon as I walked into the kitchen. "What's the matter, Michael?"

"I went out and got the mail. There's a letter from the Selective Service."

Her face went pale. "Oh no!" she cried. "Your father is already in Thailand. Now they want you too?"

I was shocked when I opened it. I was a bit naïve at that age and, for some stupid reason, under the impression that the draft just didn't apply to me. Sure, I had registered when I turned eighteen, but they would never call me. Why would they?

The draft was for the other guys, not me.

I lay in bed that night, staring at the ceiling, wondering what had happened. I knew that to be drafted meant that I would spend the remainder of my teenage years fighting a war. I had no interest in politics, political parties, or ideologies. I don't think I even knew what ideology meant. I was perfectly happy with my little diesel-stink job. I was perfectly happy with my old '62 VW that I had to park up on the sidewalk so that, in the mornings, I could push start it downhill, from the curb to the street. I was perfectly happy in my relationship with Linda, the cashier at the truck stop.

She didn't date teenage boys, though.

I watched the mail very closely for several days after that, halfway expecting a letter of apology and a retraction from the draft board, admitting that they had made a mistake.

Nothing ever came.

Unfortunately, it *was* me they had chosen to fight a war. I had been selected to have an arm blown off, or maybe a leg. I had been picked to die in a swampy rice paddy while little gook guys stared down at my body—poking me with their bayonets to see if I was really dead.

I had been chosen to go to war. Just like that, my passport to a happy, carefree teenage life had been revoked.

∎

It was a bright and sunny Monday morning in early July of 1969. The weekend was over, and the downtown area was bustling with activity. The small bus station in Laurel, Maryland, was packed with young men milling about, talking to their families, and trying not to think of the future. Some were sad, some were quiet, and some were exuding an air of false bravado. The next bus would arrive in thirty minutes. My mother and two younger sisters, dressed in their Sunday best, accompanied me as we stood outside on the sidewalk. None of us spoke very much. I tried my best to be brave. No one wanted to be the first to burst into tears.

"Are you going to be OK?" my mother asked for the umpteenth time.

I gave her a hug. "Mom, I'm not going off to war. I'm just going to boot camp. I'll be fine."

"OK, OK," she smiled meekly, knowing full well that boot camp was but a precursor to Vietnam.

The harried ticket agent announced the bus arrival over the loudspeaker.

"Time to go, Mom."

"I know," she said and bit her lip as a tear traced her cheek.

The bus pulled up close to the sidewalk. Young men swarmed out from all corners of the bus station and slowly boarded. I found a seat in the very back.

My last memory of home was looking out the back window at my mother and sisters waving as the bus disappeared down the road. My mother was dabbing at her eyes. My little sisters were too young to comprehend the gravity of the situation. They became but tiny specks in the distance.

Would it be the last time I ever saw them?

During the bus ride, I sat and watched the scenery pass by my window. As much as I did not want to go, I still felt a sense of duty to serve my country. My father had been in the Army for over twenty years. It was only fitting that I followed in his footsteps.

We arrived at the Induction Center in Richmond, Virginia, three hours later. The driver pulled up alongside a large red brick auditorium-style building. A large, mean-looking sergeant boarded the bus and glared at us, his eyes spitting fire from hell.

"Get off the damn bus, you scum. Now! Get off! Get off!"

"Get your ass off the damn bus. Move! Move! Move!"

I quickly scrambled off the bus and joined a large contingent of other young draftees standing around in a big room. We were taken out into a cavernous hallway and told to line up against the wall. A fleeting image of a firing squad danced across my mind, but then reality set in. There was nothing funny about this.

I was going into the military.

After all the recruits were lined up, a burly sergeant came out and walked down to the far end of the line. He reminded me of a grizzly bear in a uniform. Most of the young men weren't paying much attention. They were either nervously conversing amongst themselves or staring down at the floor, lost in thought.

I watched the big sergeant closely. He was counting heads and moving some of the boys to the other side of the hall. I couldn't hear what he was saying, but I kept my eyes on him, determined to figure out what was going to transpire.

I had always regarded myself as relatively attentive. Not that I was smarter than anyone else, I just seemed to notice things. My earliest memory of intuitive ability was probably in elementary school. Belinda Thompson was the princess of the third grade, and she knew it. During the recess period, she would sit in the middle of the merry-go-round and make all of us boys push her around, tilting her head back so that her bright blonde curls blew with the wind. It was always the same game every day: she was the Queen of England, and we were her knaves.

Push—Push harder!

At the end of the recess period, she would always reward one lucky boy with a kiss on the cheek. She was well aware that—for the promise of a kiss—she could get all the boys in class to push her around, day after day, week after week, month after month. I figured out very soon what was going on. The rest were all dumbstruck by her charm.

I still pushed her, though. After all, a kiss is a kiss.

Belinda Thompson... Belinda Thompson... I never did get a kiss. I wonder why. Maybe I never pushed hard enough. Or perhaps she knew that I had figured out her little playground scam.

... Oh my God! How stupid of me. I caught myself staring down at the floor, lost in my thoughts—thoughts of Belinda Thompson—thoughts of a kiss from the past... I had become another poor recruit standing in line against the wall. I shook my head, trying to clear my brain. I didn't know how long I had been daydreaming or what I had missed. I did not know where the sergeant was, what he was doing, or what was going on.

I looked up the line. I was relieved to see that he was still down the hall a bit. He was still moving people to the other side. I breathed a little easier.

As he got closer, I could hear him bark clearly. "One, two, three—Marine. One, two, three—Marine."

Every third man was going to the Marines Corps.

At once, I started counting the men ahead of me. One, two, three. One, two, three. One, two, three. When number three landed on me, I panicked. I did a quick recount. It had to be wrong. Unfortunately, the recount confirmed my worst fear. I felt blood rushing to my head. I thought I might pass out. I thought of all the newscasts I had been watching every night, documenting the Marine losses in Vietnam. Under no circumstances did I want to be a Marine—none.

I looked around for an exit door.

Then, quick-witted, I turned to the recruit to the left of me. "Hey, huh... I wonder if you'd mind changing places with me. I'd like to talk to the guy on the other side of you. We met on the bus ride down here from Maryland."

"Yeah, sure. Not a problem."

A few minutes later, the big sergeant came by. "One, two, three—Marine."

I was number two.

I often thought of the poor young Marine—number three—during my stint in the Army. I felt terrible at times, thinking about what I had done. Sometimes I would sit by myself and contemplate how such an innocent, foolish, and selfish spur-of-the-moment act could have such a profound impact on someone's life.

Guilt was my frequent companion.

In 1969 the percentage of Marines going to Vietnam was probably 100. The portion who returned home was considerably lower. Did the poor young Marine end up in a muddy rice paddy somewhere, the victim of a Viet Cong bullet? I wondered if he had regretted changing places with me that day as he lay there staring at the sky, gasping for his last breath of air.

Not a problem, he had said. *Not a problem.*

Those words haunted me for many years.

I hope he survived his tour in Vietnam. I hope he's sitting around the bar in some American Legion hall somewhere, telling everyone the story of how he was supposed to have been in the Army, but some jerk in line made him change places, and he got picked for the Marines.

I hope he is alive and well.

•

Basic training at Fort Bragg, North Carolina, consisted of misery, misery, and more misery. The heat, humidity, and mosquitoes of late summer were at times unbearable.

I prayed for rain, but it never seemed to come.

Basic Training is pure hell. Basic Training in August is pure hell times two. It's even worse when you're not that good at all of the intense physical training. I never played football, never practiced sit-ups in the backyard, never was a tough guy. It was all I could do most of the time just to get through the day alive. Lucky for me, though, I ran track in high school, so at least I could keep up when we had to run places, which was most of the time. I wasn't the worst trainee by any means. I would place myself in the middle somewhere, I guess.

The worst was Sinkmeyer.

In every military unit, there is someone who just does not fit in. My company was no different. Sam Sinkmeyer was one of those people who just plain aggravated everybody he met. He was from the Bronx, the son of a wealthy jeweler, and he had been drafted. He was a pale-skinned kid, a bit overweight, and his hair appeared to be prematurely thinning. His thick, bushy eyebrows gave way to a large Jimmy Durante-style nose, making him appear older than he really was. He was always the last one to finish when we had to run anywhere. He was the last one climbing the training walls, the worst on the rifle range, and he always got beat up in the hand-to-hand combat drills. He was the worst in everything. Nobody liked him, and every night when he went to climb into his bunk, he found his bed short-sheeted, where the bottom sheet is folded in half, making it impossible to get into bed. It's probably the worst thing that can happen to a poor recruit in boot camp. Coming back from a day of training, exercising, and misery, all a recruit has to look forward to is crawling into that pathetic little bunk. To have it end up sub-standard in any way is just unacceptable. After a week, Sinkmeyer gave up and just started sleeping on the top of his bunk.

Fort Bragg is, without a doubt, the pine tree capital of the world. The tall, scraggly cone-laden trees were everywhere. The smell of pine was everywhere. The morning smelled like pine, as did the afternoon and the evenings. To this day, I hate pine trees.

Our drill instructors seemed to delight in making us as miserable as possible by deliberately humiliating us. Nobody was addressed by their name. We were called every bad name imaginable, even some that were unimaginable. I suppose it was meant to break us down and form us into a lean, mean, fighting force, but it just led me to hate the men training me.

The worst part of basic training was being woken up at 4:30 AM by the drill instructor flipping on all the bright fluorescent lights in the barracks. There were enough of them in our building to illuminate a small town. They were the brightest lights in the world and startled me awake every morning. I hated that more than anything.

Rigorous physical training became my daily schedule. Preparing for the strains of eventual combat was difficult. I was not ready to face the strict daily routine and workout imposed by basic training. A 5:30 AM formation in the company area was followed by calisthenics and running, after which the recruits went to breakfast—*if* they could cross the monkey bars.

I was a bit on the scrawny side, and my greatest fear was the monkey bar set that had to be traversed hand-over-hand to get into the mess hall. There were three sets of them, twenty feet each in length. Recruits were required to swing down one set, up the other, down the third, then into the chow hall. Fall off, and it's back to the beginning.

I missed several meals during basic training because of those damn bars.

We were allotted five minutes for each meal: breakfast, lunch, and dinner. The drill instructors were always present to make sure no one got too comfortable.

"Hurry up and eat and get the hell out."

I remember one incident in particular. The mess hall had meatloaf for dinner—my favorite—although it was far from being any good. I tried to enjoy it anyway. It must have been over the 5-minute limit because one of the drill sergeants came by my table, stopped in front of me, and swiftly backhanded my tray of food onto the floor.

"I said, hurry up and eat and get the hell out!"

We had three drill instructors, one of whom we never saw except at formations and special events. The other two were a constant pain in the ass. Both were former Army Rangers who seemed to enjoy making our lives as miserable as possible. One of them, the younger of the two, was a Spec-4 but was in an E-5, or sergeant, slot. Although he was only an acting sergeant, he really enjoyed being called "sergeant."

The US Army permitted us nothing in Basic Training. Uncle Sam would provide all we would ever need.

Except for an ice-cold Coca-Cola.

One night our platoon was getting ready for lights out, which was at nine o'clock. We had close to 45 minutes remaining, and someone came up with the idea of sending out for cokes, which was utterly forbidden. The snack bar was two blocks over and was open until 10:00 p.m. Of course, it was off-limits to recruits. We drew toothpicks to see who the lucky runner would be. One toothpick had been broken in half.

I picked it.

I was sneaking around the darkened corner of the barracks with six large cokes in my hands when I heard a noise behind me. "Where do you think you're going, dumbass?"

I froze and slowly turned around to see the smiling face of the Spec-4 drill sergeant.

He ordered me to follow him to the drill sergeant's office.

"You can just set all those cokes right on that desk, dumb shit."

"Would you rather I poured them all out, Sarge?" I asked. "No, stupid ass, you must be very thirsty. Start drinking," he commanded.

"Sarge, there are six of them." I protested.

"Too bad. Get started."

I got through Coca-Cola number four before I had to run to the door. Rushing outside, they all came back up. I felt miserable.

"I just can't drink anymore, Sarge," I pleaded.

"Well, that's too bad, shithead. You've still got two more to go."

Needless to say, to this day, I still harbor a loathing for drill sergeants.

.

Fireguard duty was a nightly ritual. Two recruits had to patrol the barracks area watching for fires and cleaning whatever needed cleaning. Staying awake in the middle of the night for the two-hour shifts was very difficult.

Getting caught sleeping during fireguard was out of the question.

I remember one particular night when I was walking amongst the bunks, arranged in neat order on the second floor of the barracks, when I spied a candy wrapper on the floor, right next to Sinkmeyer's bed. Candy was a no-no in basic, along with everything else. I thought about the situation for a moment, then reached down and picked up the wrapper. Having candy in basic was akin to committing a felony. There was no sense in having Sinkmeyer get in trouble for that. His life, as a struggling recruit, was difficult enough.

In 1969 there was a long-serving congressman from Louisiana named F. Edward Hebert. I'd never met the man, but we shared the same unusual last name. One hot morning we were all standing in formation sweating, waiting to catch hell for something, as was the norm.

The assistant DI, the Spec 4, eased his way through the formation and wound up in front of me—his face mere inches from my own.

"Dirtbag, dumbass," he whispered. "I saw something in the paper this morning about some big shot Washington senator also named Hebert. Any relation to you?"

I didn't know what to say, but something in my head told me that this might be an opportunity.

I hesitated—just long enough for effect—then bellowed, "I can't say, Drill Sergeant!"

He stared at me for a moment, and then a knowing smirk spread across his face. He turned and walked away.

Less than twenty-four hours later, word had spread throughout the training company that I was related to a big-shot senator, that he was probably an uncle or something.

I never had to pull KP duty after that day.

Of course, I never confirmed or denied the association. Why kill a golden goose?

·

Towards the end of basic training, the entire company was to go on a twenty-mile march. At formation early that morning, the drill sergeant asked if anyone had experience driving a large diesel truck. The regular driver had become ill.

Probably food poisoning, I thought.

No one said a word. Looking around the formation and realizing a possible opportunity, my hand shot up.

"I've had experience driving tractor-trailers, Sarge."

While not exactly an untruth, I suppose I should have mentioned that it was only in the parking lot of a truck stop.

I was directed to the mess hall and found myself the proud new operator of a multi-fuel 2½-ton truck loaded with food and water. I was to drive the mess truck on the long, hot march.

The company of soldiers headed off down the dusty North Carolina road loaded down with their heavy backpacks and M-14 rifles. It was a typical day in Fort Bragg, sweltering and very humid. The soldiers were soaked in sweat. As they trudged down the sandy dirt road, clouds of dust wafted up from the column and just hung in mid-air, like a mirage. I was thankful that at least I was sitting in the cab of a truck and not marching down a hot, dry, and dreary road.

One morning there was a lot of commotion going on in the barracks. A group of recruits was huddled around a few of the bunks engaged in animated conversation.

"What's up?" I asked the guy in the bunk beneath mine. I wasn't all that fond of the top bunk, but there wasn't much I could do about it. All the lower ones had been taken before I could claim one.

"There's a rumor going around that we're all going to the 82nd Airborne Division after basic. They need people real bad to jump out of airplanes in Vietnam."

"Yeah," another added. "They're losing them as fast as they can replace them."

I was not pleased with this news, true or not. Rumors were rampant within the company all during basic, including the one about the guy over in Charlie Company who drank an entire can of Brasso so that he could get discharged from the Army as a whacko. I never did know if that was true or not—didn't much care, though.

After much thought and a few sleepless nights of worry, I decided that I had to do something to take a bit of control over my future... my life.

After morning formation a few days later, I approached one of my drill sergeants and inquired about the probability of us being sent to the 82nd Airborne Division.

"Pretty good," replied the DI. "They're headquartered right here at Bragg, so it would be a lot easier for all concerned if we just sent you all over there after basic."

"Is there any way out of that?" I asked.

"Sure," came the reply from the smiling DI. "All you gotta do is sign up for a third year instead of the two you got drafted for, and we'll send you to a school of your choice."

Sold! I signed on for a third year the following day. I flipped through the sizeable loose-leaf binder my first sergeant was showing me. It had listings of all the jobs in the Army. Having had "experience" only with trucks, I decided to sign up for Truck School.

"That one's full. Everybody wants to drive trucks." the sergeant bellowed.

Continuing to scan through the selections, I came upon Cooking School. My father had been a cook in the Korean War, and he had survived that just fine.

"I'll try that," I said.

"That's full, too. Everyone wants to be a cook."

Flipping through more pages, I came upon various exciting and rewarding positions: Combat Engineer, Demolition Diver, Forward Observer, Helicopter Door Gunner, Infantryman, Mortar Operator, Ranger, Sniper, Tank Driver—every one of which screamed "death-death-death" to me.

No, No, No!

I had looked through just about the entire book and was in the "W" section when something caught my eye: Watercraft Operator.

Hmmm.... I thought. *How bad could THAT be?*

"How about this one, sergeant?"

.

I arrived for Basic Seaman Course soon after that. Fort Eustis, Virginia, was located on the banks of the James River, near Jamestown and Williamsburg. It was a much greener area with fewer pine trees. The Basic Seaman Course consisted of more physical training and learning how to tie lines, splice steel cables, chipping paint, and other deckhand-related duties.

Twelve weeks later, I was nearing the completion of my training. The instructors advanced the top 5% of the class to the next level or Crewman Course. Having never been an outstanding student, I was a bit surprised and pleased to learn that I was one of those selected.

I was worried about placing in the top 10% of the second class. Those who didn't make the cut were sent out into the service as deckhands on tugs, landing craft, or other types of boats. After several weeks of the Crewman Course, I advanced to the Harbor Craft Operator Course.

I enjoyed learning how to operate and maneuver different types of Army vessels. The harbor at Fort Eustis was full of landing craft, tugboats, and barges. My favorite was the LCM-8, a steel-hulled landing craft, 78 feet long, powered by four 6-71 Detroit Diesels driving twin propellers. While not very fast and looking a bit like a motorized dustpan, they were very agile and forgiving. It was quite a nimble craft.

Training at Fort Eustis, Virginia, in late fall had its good days and bad days. The year that I was there, it seemed as though winter had arrived a bit early. While training on the large tugboats was fun, it could get frigid out on the James River at times. All of the students had to take turns at the wheel, but whenever they were not piloting, everyone would crowd into the smokestack access area where it was warm. The regular tug crew occupied the mess area and other sections of the tug, and students were not permitted access.

I seemed to excel at operating the landing craft. It was kind of like a truck—just on water. I knew that my entire class was bound for Vietnam. Somehow, it didn't seem so bad, knowing that I'd be on a landing craft. I hoped that I wouldn't get assigned to an LCU, though, a larger, lumbering landing craft that was quite possibly the slowest boat in the world. They were nothing but a big, slow target.

Graduation for the Harbor Craft Operator course was in early November. I was given a 30-day pass before being shipped to Vietnam. I went home for a welcome visit with the family.

.

A month later, I found myself strapped into my seat, feeling the rumbling of the wheels on the tarmac as the big Capitol Airways 707 jet screamed down the runway. Shortly after takeoff, I felt the familiar "thump-thump" of the wheels retracting into their respective bays. The young G.I. seated next to me jumped.

"First time flying?" I asked.

"Yes," came the nervous reply.

As the plane gained altitude, I settled in for the long haul across the Pacific. The jet had taken off from McChord Air Force Base in Tacoma, Washington. It was bound for a refueling stop in Anchorage, Alaska, then Yokota, Japan, before delivering us all to Bien Hoa Air Base, Vietnam.

Seated in a center seat, I introduced myself to the soldiers on either side of me. The one next to the window, a PFC, while the same age as me, looked much younger.

I dubbed him "The Kid."

It was amazing how quiet the plane was, considering over 200 teenage soldiers were on board. Most, like me, were probably apprehensive about the flight since just a few weeks earlier, an identical Capitol Airways flight with 219 soldiers and airmen aboard had crashed in Anchorage after a refueling stop. Forty-six young GI's and one flight attendant were killed in the raging inferno after the plane exploded in flames on the runway. I tried not to think of the event as our flight lifted off from Anchorage. I was happy that it had been dark outside so that any remaining wreckage—if there was any—would not be visible. I thought how sad it was for those poor young men to have died on their way to war.

Dozing off for a few moments, the sound of faint sobbing nearby woke me. I looked over at the young GI. I could see the unmistakable traces of tears running down his cheeks.

I looked at him and wondered what the hell his problem was. The kid was sitting there, sobbing quietly to himself.

I thought about shaking some sense into him. *Get a hold of yourself, kid! What's your problem? We're all in the same boat here.*

After some time, compassion replaced contempt, and I tried my best to make conversation and calm him down a bit. His name was Jesse Griggs. He was fresh out of high school, a farm kid from Idaho. Not only was this his first plane ride, but it was also his first time away from home.

The Jessie kid was positive that he was on his way to certain death in a far-away land, fighting in a war nobody cared about. He told me how much he missed his mother, father, brothers, and sister. To make matters worse, I found out the kid was Infantry, possibly the worst duty assignment in Vietnam. He had been drafted, and he was scared, scared to death.

Every time I looked over at him, he seemed to be in tears.

Flying high above the Pacific Ocean gave me plenty of time to contemplate: my life, my home, my future, everything. It didn't take me long to conclude that signing up for a third year in the Army was probably the wisest decision I had ever made. I could have gambled on my future and just gone in as a draftee for two years. Maybe they would have sent me to a school of some type anyway. Maybe not. I couldn't envision myself humping through the jungle with 50 pounds of gear slung on my back. No, it wasn't worth the gamble.

Sign up for just one extra year of your life and go to the school of your choice. What a deal!

I sat back in my seat and thought about all the other times I had flown. With a father in the military, our family had traveled quite a bit. I noticed how all the details that usually made travel so enjoyable were absent on this plane. Everyone looked the same: same uniform, same haircut, same shoes... same forlorn look of impending doom on their faces.

The aircraft eventually landed at Bien Hoa Air Base and taxied to the appropriate area.

The flight attendant came on the PA. "Gentlemen, we have landed in Vietnam. Please make your way to the front exit door."

Nobody moved. A stagnant silence fell over the plane. Nobody seemed very anxious to get up out of their seats. It seemed so surreal. We had arrived at our destination.

Vietnam.

Gradually, one by one, some of the soldiers quietly started making their way up the aisle.

I wondered which ones were walking to their death.

When I approached the front, I turned to exit the plane and was greeted in the open doorway with what seemed like a blow torch of hot air—the hottest I had ever felt. It was hot in Vietnam. Very, very hot. The humidity was unlike anything else known to mankind. I paused for a moment in the doorway of the plane.

Had we just landed in hell?

Young Jesse Griggs and I shook hands and parted ways. By this time, the kid even had me convinced that he would die in the jungle, probably alone. As I watched him walk away, a feeling of sorrow came over me. I didn't know what else I could have done. I just felt as though I hadn't done quite enough to help him.

∎

The deafening roar of a helicopter coming in for a landing on the helipad next door woke me with a start. For a few moments, I was disoriented, unsure of where I was. Then it hit me; I had arrived in Vietnam. It was January the sixth, 1970, my first full day in country. I was in a strange bed. The mattress was skimpy, the OD green Army blanket even skimpier. I was overcome by an overwhelming sense of loneliness, despair, and fear. Even though I was surrounded by hundreds of others just like me, I felt terribly alone. I felt like I would be alone forever. I was to be in this war zone for one year. One year was an eternity. I remember lying in my bed, staring at the little coiled springs under the bunk above me. There seemed to be a million of them.

Up to this point in my life, I had never realized that fear could be so consuming and intense. I had experienced what I had thought to be fear before: I feared my father coming home after I had done something wrong; I feared not having completed my homework for Mrs. McKenzie's class; I even feared the dog next door.

This, however, was a fear that I had never experienced before, and it terrified me. I was in Vietnam. And I was sure that I was going to die there. Day one of 365. Would I wake to this fear each and every day? Only time would tell. I was not prepared to fight in a war. I was just a kid. How would I react in combat? How would I react when that first bullet came flying towards me? Suppose I froze on the battlefield?

Terror gripped my soul. I wondered how I might borrow some courage from someone.

I prayed... and prayed some more. I promised God that if he'd get me out of this alive, with two arms, two legs, ten fingers, and ten toes, that I'd devote the rest of my life to becoming a better person. I felt like I wanted to cry. I probably would have had I been alone, but then I remembered the kid from the plane—Jesse Griggs—and forced myself to regain my composure.

The sounds of war were all around me—jeeps whizzing about, engines revving to high rpm's, trucks carrying supplies, helicopters going in all different directions all at once. I was both frightened and fascinated at the same time.

I listened to planes taking off and others landing. In the far distance, I could hear the haunting sounds of war—*Boom! Boom! Boom!* Artillery rounds were landing far off in the distance. I hoped somebody wasn't getting killed somewhere. There were soldiers everywhere. Some, like me, in brand-new fatigues, others—the old-timers—in faded and wrinkled ones, worn out from many months at war. The guys who had been in-country a long time tended to treat the newcomers like dirt. They had all forgotten that they, too, had been new at one time.

They called us FNG's.

What the hell did that mean?

■

I was standing in a formation on the parade field at the 90th Replacement Battalion in Long Binh. I was surrounded by young boys, fresh out of high school—several hundred of us—all new arrivals, all dressed in new olive drab green uniforms, all waiting to find out where we would be assigned. I didn't associate with any of them as it didn't seem healthy to make new friends or learn someone's name.

Tomorrow they might be dead.

The heat was unbearable. The sun and humidity were unrelenting, making my newly-issued jungle fatigues feel like wet rags.

The sergeant on the podium called out names, sometimes several at a time, and directed the soldiers off to an area at the side of the formation where a representative from their new units met them. This process seemed to take forever. I was getting anxious. To which landing craft unit would I be assigned? Several were operating in Vietnam.

"Specialist Four Michael Hebert, 92nd Military Police Battalion," yelled the sergeant on the podium as he pointed to an area for me to report. There was an MP standing there.

I just stared at him. "What?" I exclaimed to the G.I. next to me. "Are they crazy? I'm a boat operator, not an MP. How did they manage to get that all screwed up?"

I hoisted my duffel bag and slowly walked over to the MP.

"Hi, I'm Sgt. Sweeney," he said, extending his hand.

I introduced myself, shook his hand, and followed him to his jeep.

"Hop in. We've got a bit of a drive. We have to go to the other side of the city, so relax and get comfortable."

I threw my duffle bag in the back seat and hoisted myself into the little jeep. A 'Military Police' decal was visible across the front of the windshield.

Highway QL-1, Long Binh

We drove through the main gate at Long Binh and turned onto a busy two-lane highway. The road was full of Army trucks, jeeps, little French Renaults, pedicabs, and motorbikes—hundreds of them. Everybody was in a hurry to get somewhere.

"I'm not an MP," I informed Sweeney as we headed south down Highway QL-1 towards Saigon. "I have no idea why they assigned me to an MP Battalion. I'm a boat coxswain. I drive boats."

"That's what you're going to do," Sweeney explained, "You're getting assigned to the 458th Transportation Company or 458th PBRs for short, and they're attached to us: the 18th MP Brigade of the 92nd MP Battalion."

"What?" I asked. "What is a PBR? I'm supposed to be on a landing craft. That's what I trained for."

"It's a River Patrol Boat," said Sweeney. "You must be an emergency replacement or something. They've been short of coxswains for a while now."

"Well, I wish someone had told me about it before this. I have no idea what's going on."

"Just don't worry about it. You'll find out soon enough."

I sat back in the seat, my mind spinning. My comfortable image of how I would spend my year in Viet Nam was upside down. I had never heard of a PBR before. I resigned that I would have to wait and find out what was going on when we got to wherever we were going.

We were approaching downtown Saigon. I was very apprehensive as we turned down one street after another, and traffic slowed to a crawl. Having never been in a war zone before, I was half expecting people to be shooting at me from the moment I arrived. I spent an inordinate amount of time looking around and watching the rooftops, looking for anyone with a weapon pointed in our direction.

Sweeney noticed my concern and leaned towards me with a smile. "Calm down, man. No one's going to shoot you here!"

Saigon Street

Saigon was a city in utter chaos. Maybe chaos is too kind a word. Traffic going through downtown was an absolute free-for-all. I had never seen or heard anything like it in my entire life. It was a cacophony of madness, madness with a distinct electric feeling about it, however. The blast of noise and traffic was overwhelming. Vehicles were careening everywhere. Little French cars, panel trucks, taxis, motorcycles, pedicabs, and bicycles jammed the streets, all jockeying for a bit of pavement. They were everywhere, whizzing in and out of traffic. Nobody yielded to anyone.

The clatter of cars, bikes, and mopeds rumbling over the rustic cobblestone streets filled the air. The shouts of merchants hawking their wares became louder and louder as we approached the center of the shopping district. People walked down the middle of the street, oblivious to the surrounding traffic.

Saigon Shops

The afternoon heat brought more putrid smells to life than I needed, smells of every imaginable kind. Every street had a different, distinct odor, some sweet, some pungent, some dirty, and some downright stinky—gasoline, garbage, raw sewage, and then food stalls—each sending my senses into overload. The smells were something I would never forget.

Most of the streets were packed to capacity. It was nothing to see a motorbike zip up onto the sidewalk and try to weave amongst the crowds. I couldn't believe they didn't all run into each other. It almost seemed like a choreographed dance of sorts—albeit a really crazy one. It was such a shock having just come from Maryland where order was the norm: these cars went that way; those cars went this way. People walked on this sidewalk going that way, others on the other sidewalk going the other way. Mopeds were not allowed on the roads. Motorcycles followed the cars in a neat and orderly line—period. This, however, was totally different.

I just gawked at them all.

Family Transportation

Everything was abuzz with activity. It was the middle of the afternoon. Shops were open all along both sides of the streets, in addition to an overabundance of fruit and vegetable stands and other little carts selling just about anything one could imagine. I spied one old lady squatting on the sidewalk between two large straw baskets connected to a pole, which I assumed she used to transport her goods. She had a pile of paper plates next to her.

"She's selling chicken and rice," Sweeney said. "Chicken in one basket, rice in the other."

I was watching her with interest when I saw her smile at a customer.

"Her teeth are all black!" I said to Sweeney.

"Yeah, you'll see a lot of that here. Lots of the older people do it. It's from chewing Betel Nut. It's kind of like a stimulant. Supposedly, it reduces the pain of gum disease."

I took it all in—a new kid in a new town. I could not recall ever having seen so many people in one place before. The city was alive, vibrant, hectic, and crowded, yet a distinct aura of sadness seemed to filter through.

People were rushing and hustling around. They seemed indifferent to the war surrounding them.

Nothing seemed safe or sacred.

We were slowly making our way down a heavily-traveled street somewhere near the middle of the city. The jeep was just crawling along. Sweeney was steering with one hand, the other resting on the windshield frame.

All of a sudden, I heard him yell, "I'll be damned! That little kid just jerked my watch right off my arm."

Sweeney slammed on the brakes, stood halfway up in the seat, unhooked the flap of his holster, and pulled out his .45 caliber pistol. I had no idea what was going on. Before I could even react, Sweeney jacked the slide back and fired his gun, the bullet striking the rear end of an old French Citroën 2CV parked nearby.

Twang!

As soon as the shot rang out, people panicked and started to scatter, running in all different directions. Some who had witnessed the events unfold, however, just stopped and watched.

"*Den day,*" Sweeney yelled. "Come here!"

A young boy, about 10 or 11, emerged from behind the car, holding a wristwatch in his hand. He was a scruffy little kid, one of the Saigon street orphans. His hair hadn't been combed in weeks, maybe months, and he wore a tattered old long-sleeved white shirt which had probably been scrounged from a rubbish bin somewhere. His torn and dirty short pants rounded out his outfit. Like most of the orphans roaming the streets of Saigon, he was barefoot. He raised his hands over his head, crept up to the jeep, and handed Sweeney the watch. Sweeney grabbed it from his hand and then placed the barrel of the .45 on the child's forehead, right between his eyes.

He didn't say a word. He just stared at the child.

The boy started to tremble as his eyes filled with tears.

A small crowd had gathered nearby, hoping not to witness the horrific execution of a poor orphan street urchin. I noticed several other young boys standing half a block away, all older than this one, watching with great interest. I wondered if they had put him up to this, perhaps on a dare?

Some of the older Vietnamese women nearby were visibly distraught, wailing and holding their hands up to their faces in shock. The men in attendance were standing at a distance, staring in disbelief. None would dare intervene. They were all intimidated by the MP armband on Sweeney's left sleeve, his jet-black MP helmet, and the 'Military Police' decal splashed across the front of the windshield.

They all knew there was nothing they could do to save the young boy.

Sweeney was just staring at the boy; the .45 pressed firmly into his forehead, the red impression from the gun barrel growing larger and larger. His finger twitched on the trigger several times.

I just sat there, looking at all the bystanders, wondering what I should do. Interfering in a Military Police affair did not seem like a wise move on my first day in-country.

Somehow, though, it didn't seem to matter.

"No!" I cried out. "It's just a watch. Let him go."

Sweeney thought for a moment, staring at the terrorized young boy. He withdrew his pistol from the child's head and shoved it into his holster.

"*Di di mau!*" he yelled, commanding the boy to go. He put the watch, now with a broken band, in his pocket and sat back down in the seat. He glanced over at me as he put the jeep in gear.

"Hell, man," he grinned, "I wouldn't have shot the kid—just wanted to put the fear into him."

Oh great, I thought, as I let out a silent sigh of relief, not quite believing the fiasco I had just been a party to.

Welcome to Vietnam.

Downtown Saigon

We continued making our way through the city without further incident, arriving at last outside a gated and guarded compound situated at the far end of Tan Son Nhut Air Base.

"This is Pershing Field," Sweeney explained. "It's the Battalion Headquarters for the Military Police."

It was also the Company Headquarters for the 458th River Patrol Boat unit, or Sea Tigers, as indicated by the sign out front.

I looked all around as the jeep entered the compound. It was a small place. There was a soccer field next door.

There were no boats anywhere in sight...

I stayed at the compound for several days. I visited the tiny barbershop near the barracks and got a haircut from a little old Vietnamese lady who spoke no English. Finishing with my trim, she motioned for me to lean forward, and then she put her hands together as if in prayer. What happened next shocked me. She beat her hands all up and down my back, making little 'cracking' noises. It felt wonderful! After several minutes of that, I felt like a new man. I gave her a very good tip.

The boats were all down at the river, I was told, at a place called Newport, several miles away. It didn't look like I was going to visit there any time soon. They seemed to be trying to find a place to put me. I had still yet to even see a PBR. Meanwhile, I was issued an M-16 rifle, helmet, flak vest, and other accouterments of a soldier at war. What would become my favorite item, however, I had to purchase from a nearby shop. It turned out that the 458th Sea Tigers was somewhat of an elite unit, the only one of its kind in the entire United States Army. They were authorized, along with the associated MP personnel, to wear the coveted black beret, and I gently placed one on my head with pride.

The Executive Officer took me aside one afternoon and explained the company to me. "They originally sent us over here to operate amphibious craft, unloading ships and cargo. Somewhere along the way, we got tapped to do patrol duty with some Boston Whaler outboard boats; the next thing you know, we've got 39 River Patrol Boats, 18 Boston Whalers, and 160 of us scattered around nine outposts all over the country. The mission now includes port and harbor security as well as armed escort of waterborne convoys. Most of our duty is performed on the rivers, but we have three seaport bases, Qui Nhon, Vung Ro Bay, and Cat Lo. Even though we're a transportation outfit, we're attached to the 18th MP Brigade. All of our boats have MPs aboard to handle the weapons. We just run the boats; we're not cops."

A couple of days later, I picked up my duffel bag and my orders and walked outside for my ride to the airport. I got into a jeep with that same idiot Sweeney.

"Hope we don't have to shoot anybody today," I quipped.

Sweeney smiled and patted the holster of his .45 caliber pistol. "I've still got my Seiko, don't I?"

■

A couple of hours later, I boarded a lumbering C-130 cargo plane full of soldiers going to Tuy Hoa in Phu Yen Province, about 375 kilometers northeast of Saigon. I found a seat halfway back down the starboard fuselage side. The seats were made of rope, like the paratroopers used: one row down either side of the plane, then two rows back-to-back down the center. They were not made for comfort.

Apparently, US-allied forces were permitted to fly on our aircraft while in-country since I found myself seated between a South Korean who had been eating kimchi, a spicy fermented side dish, and a South Vietnamese soldier who had been eating something with lots of nuoc mam, the highly aromatic fish sauce they seemed to put on everything. The stench was unbearable, and the heat inside the plane just made matters worse.

The plane took off, rumbling and shaking down the runway. All of the rope seats swung towards the back at the same time. The fully-loaded aircraft almost seemed too heavy to lift off. Still, eventually, it did, quickly gaining enough altitude to avoid any enemy snipers in the area who might want to take a shot at us.

The flight up the coast offered plenty of time for reflection, and I was lost in thought for a large part of the journey. The cooler air at higher altitude was a welcome relief. I wondered what I could have done differently. I suppose I could have gone to college and become an officer. I could have picked a different Army specialty instead of boats or even packed up and moved to Canada and avoided the draft altogether.

"No, it is what it is," I decided. First of all, I had barely scraped through high school, so college was out of the question. I enjoyed the boat training and was good at it. I would wait and make up my mind about this PBR thing. And Canada was out—it had never even crossed my mind back home. Besides, my career Army father would have killed me. He fought in the Pacific during World War II, then in Korea, and two tours of Vietnam. No, Canada was never an option.

I leaned back in my rope seat and thought about my father. He was in the US Army's Military Intelligence and had come to Vietnam in 1957 as an advisor. He liked to tell me stories of how he never wore a uniform the entire time he was in-country. He would go around in slacks and a short-sleeve shirt. Sometimes, he would wear a suit. He lived in a hotel in downtown Saigon and liked to brag about how he always did his own laundry—in the shower! He would soap up with all his clothes on, scrub around a bit, rinse off, then take his clothes off and get a shower. He would then hang his fresh-washed outfit up to dry overnight.

One of his favorite stories dealt with an assassination attempt that he had survived soon after his arrival. He was up in the highlands for an interrogation assignment and needed to get to an airport to hop a flight back to Saigon. Walking out the front door of his hotel, he hailed a 3-

wheeled Vespa motor scooter taxi with a small open-air carriage behind. He told the driver to take him to the airport and jumped in the back. The driver then sped off down the road with my father hanging on to the canopy for support. A short time later, they came to a bend in the road coming down a steep hill. There was a cliff beyond the curve. My father told me that he sensed something was wrong when the driver suddenly jumped out. At just the right moment, my father threw himself out the back as the little Vespa careened off the cliff.

The taxi driver was a Viet Cong.

Now, here I was, some twelve years later, on a C-130 cargo plane flying in the same country fighting the same damn war, assigned to some kind of boat that I'd never seen, much less even heard of. We were bound for someplace called Tuy Hoa, halfway up the coast of Vietnam and much closer to North Vietnam than I wanted to be.

I had a general idea of what the boat was, having seen an image of one painted on the sign in front of Saigon company headquarters. I also had an image of one on my river patrol boat pocket patch, which I had added to my uniform while at Pershing Field.

It was a very poor rendition of the boat, though. It just looked like a blob.

I found out from some of the others at Pershing Field that everyone assigned to the PBR boats had first been trained at the Naval Inshore Operations Training Facility in Mare Island, California.

I wondered why the Army hadn't sent me there. Everyone else had been trained in operations, tactics, weapons, and everything else they needed to know. I knew nothing, nothing at all, and frankly, I worried about going into this job cold. I didn't even know how to start the thing, never mind maneuver it or, God forbid, engage in combat at its helm.

What a debacle this was going to be!

458ᵗʰ PBR unit patch

3. Welcome to Vung Ro

It was just as hot in Tuy Hoa as it was in Saigon. The heat stole my breath away as I stepped off the back ramp of the C-130. I made my way to the check-in desk at the terminal building, gave them a copy of my orders, then walked over to where I saw two MPs waiting. "Are you guys here for Hebert?"

"Yeah. That you?"

"Yep," I replied, extending my hand. "The name's Mike Hebert, from Maryland."

"They call me Riggs," the one closest to me said, shaking my hand. "And this is the Chief."

The Chief was an American Indian—a very, very big Indian. He was probably a bit over 6 feet tall and easily weighed 240 pounds. His body was all muscle, his biceps the size of my thighs. An eagle's claw hung from a rawhide strip around his neck, which gave him an even more menacing attitude. The Chief didn't shake my hand and never said a word. He wore dark sunglasses and a floppy OD green Boonie hat, a wide-brimmed cover commonly used by troops in South Vietnam to shade from the sun.

I was immediately intimidated.

I retrieved my duffle bag from baggage claim and followed them outside. I was a bit surprised that they picked me up in a beat-up old ¾-ton truck. I had not seen, until now, an Army vehicle in such a sad state. The OD green paint had long since faded away; the white star on the doors was barely visible. Throwing my bag in the back, I climbed up into the cab and onto the rough, torn canvas seat that had seen many, many better days. Taking quick inventory, I noticed the dash was rusty, its instrumentation sparse yet seemingly functional. The stick shift on the floor sported an upside-down hand grenade in place of a knob. *What a truck!*

Riggs popped behind the wheel while the Chief hoisted himself into the back and stretched out on one of the wooden benches. "And this," he said, patting the dash affectionately, "is Old Betsy. She's not much to look at, but she gets us where we want to go. We used to have a jeep, but it went over a cliff. Then our NCOIC stole a deuce and a half for us, but it started getting hot, so he traded it to some Navy guys for a case of steaks. The MPs eventually sent Betsy down to us."

"What's with the hand grenade?" I asked.

"It didn't have a knob when we got it, so I unscrewed the fuse out of a grenade, turned it upside down, and Presto —works great."

"Is the explosive still inside?"

"Yeah, I couldn't get that out. It'll be OK, though; just don't smoke." He laughed—but I couldn't tell if it was humor or irony.

"Where you from, Chief?" I yelled through the opening in the back of the canvas top.

"Arizona"

"Been here long?" I asked, trying to break the ice.

"Yep."

"The Chief don't talk much," Riggs explained. "You'll never get much out of him. He likes to ride with me, though. I think he gets bored back at the bay."

I looked over at Riggs. He had short dark curly hair and beady eyes that were just a little too close together. He reminded me of a used car salesman with John Lennon-style glasses.

40

"We only get to come up here once or twice a week, mostly to pick up the mail. Mail call is a very important event. Usually, we'll bring a whole truckload—whoever's not on duty—and we'll spend the day here. They've got movies, a snack bar, a PX, church; you name it."

We turned onto Highway QL-1 and headed south. Rice paddies, rich and fertile, stretched for as far as the eye could see. Visible in the far distance, vast mountain ranges rose to meet billowing white cloud formations, every so often allowing a band of golden sunlight to burst through.

I was surprised at the beauty of such a war-torn land. It was such a strange and different country.

"That's where we're going," commented Riggs, noticing where I was looking. "Vung Ro Bay is on the other side of that mountain. It's about 35 kilometers to Ca Pass. Sit back; we've got about an hour's drive."

I settled in for the ride. It was going to be an exciting adventure.

We came upon a large field with several dozen farmers harvesting rice by hand. They were all bent over, toiling in the rice paddies, their little conical hats adding a comedic atmosphere to the arduous, tiring work. Everybody worked in the fields: old men, old ladies, young children. Life seemed to be an endless struggle for these quiet, dignified people. None of them spoke as they toiled in the hot sun.

"Both the men and women wear those black silk pajama things for working in the rice paddies," Riggs told me. "They're called Ao Ba Ba's or something like that. They're very easy to wash the mud out of."

"They harvest rice twice a year in this area." he continued, slowing the truck to allow me to take it all in. "Everybody in the village is involved."

Villagers harvesting the rice crop

Quite a few water buffalo were lingering by the side of the road.

"I've never seen a water buffalo before. They're a lot bigger than I thought they would be, maybe even bigger than American buffalo. I wouldn't know, though. I've never seen one of those, either."

Riggs laughed.

We were passing a large water buffalo lingering near the roadside. At first, I thought my eyes were playing tricks on me, but then I looked harder.

"Hey! That buffalo has knives taped to his horns. What the heck is that for?"

"Whatever you do, stay well clear of that one. That's the leader of the pack, man, the boss buffalo," Riggs answered. "The knives are so that he can gorge any attackers, especially wild boar. He can tear 'em to pieces. Some of these water buffalo are mean—meaner than the Chief back there."

He went on. "You've come to a veritable zoo here, man. We've got all kinds of wild animals: tigers, elephants, rhinos, leopards, bears, and a million monkeys. Maybe two million monkeys!"

Lumbering along Highway QL-1, we passed a Korean Inspection Point but were not hampered. It was only the second time I had seen a South Korean soldier.

"I didn't know they had troops over here until I sat next to one on the plane up here."

"Yeah, man," answered Riggs. "We've got a unit stationed right above us, higher up on the mountain. They're with the White Horse Division—mean as hell too. The VC are deathly afraid of them. A few weeks ago, we were coming down the mountain from Vung Ro, and we saw seven or eight heads lined up alongside the road. The Koreans had decapitated them and put their heads on display as a warning to other VC. You'll get to meet them. They're always coming to the Bay to trade stuff with us, mostly our expended brass from the machine guns. I guess they send it home to make trinkets."

I shuddered at the thought of seven or eight heads lined up on the roadside, indeed a gruesome sight and one that I hoped never to witness.

Abandoned train station

An abandoned, bullet-riddled, and bomb-scarred building came into view.

"That used to be a train station," Riggs told me. "I think the French built it, but I'm not sure. Anyway, not much left of it now. In the early days of the war, it was bombed by American B-52s. I heard it was early in the morning, and there was a train approaching the station at the time. It got caught up in the explosion, turned over, and burst into flames. Women, children, and old men ran screaming from the carnage, their bodies on fire. The Koreans were the first on the scene, but there wasn't a whole lot they could do. They said the flames were unbelievable. I think everybody pretty much burnt up."

Shortly after passing the train station, Riggs slowed to a crawl as we approached a single-lane floating bridge constructed next to a sizeable blown-out span.

"This is the Ban Thach River. The VC blew up the main span a year or so ago. The Army Engineers put this pontoon bridge in a few weeks after. It was the best we could get, although it's a bit on the shaky side."

Pontoon Bridge on Ban Thach River

We drove up onto a steel ramp and started across the wooden decking running the length of the bridge. I looked out the window. The water was muddy brown and had a distinct odor of sewage and oil. The entire structure shook and wobbled under the weight of our truck.

"This thing won't sink, will it?" I asked.

"Hope not," Riggs replied. "It's got thirty pontoons on it."

Market day in the village

We continued down Highway QL-1. The rice paddies gave way to mountain lowlands, and as we came upon a small village, Riggs downshifted the truck and drove at a much slower pace. I was surprised to see that the people seemed to be very poor, living in homes made of just about any material they could scrounge—usually discarded wood—sometimes even cardboard. The village looked the same as it probably had for a hundred years. It would probably still look poor and ragged in another hundred years.

Vendors were lining the sides of the road with baskets full of goods. Children on bicycles had come into town, purchased what their parents had ordered, and were carefully returning home.

"It's market day," Riggs explained. "Everyone comes to town for market day."

"What kind of things do they sell here?" I asked.

"Well, you can get all kinds of stuff. These folks are mostly selling chickens, straw goods, vegetables, spices. Even drugs!"

I was fascinated by the bustling activity. Riggs drove with caution and care through the village as people were everywhere. Everybody seemed to be wearing a conical straw hat, which I found very entertaining. Riggs said they were called nón lá's.

People seemed to be trying their best to get out of our way. I had forgotten that we were in a Military Police truck. People noticed it. Riggs stopped to allow some bicycles to cross the road.

I looked out the side window. Not five feet away, an old Mama-San was sitting by the side of the road selling straw baskets and hats. She didn't even have a chair. She was just squatting.

The old lady looked wrinkled, gaunt, and tired. I suppose she had to do whatever she could to earn a living, even at her age. Our eyes met as I stared at her. At first, I misinterpreted the look as one of hatred, but then I realized it was sadness. Her desperate, mournful eyes must have been witness to a thousand stories, very few of them uplifting. She must have known many years of misery, first from the French who had occupied her country for 100 years and now by the newcomer Americans. I wondered if she ever smiled, or laughed, or even had a happy day.

Something—I'm not sure what—passed between us. An understanding, I suppose, but in that very brief moment, I somehow came to appreciate the hardships of war and the effects it had on the Vietnamese people.

"There seems to be a noticeable absence of young men around. All I see are young boys, old men, or disabled veterans."

"They've all gone off to fight the war," said Riggs. "All been drafted."

"Where are you from?" I asked.

"Well, for the past several years, I've been living on a dairy farm just outside Minneapolis. My folks were killed in a car wreck when I was fourteen, and my aunt and uncle took me in."

"Wow, I'm sorry to hear that."

"Yeah, it was a long time ago. My aunt and uncle were OK, but I think they were happy when I got drafted. They didn't have any kids, so I think I kind of got in the way, you know?"

"So, how long have you been in Vietnam?"

"I'm halfway through my second year," Riggs answered. "I've extended my tour twice now, and they just leave me right here in Vung Ro, so that suits me fine. I don't have much to go back for—got no girl, no job, no home. Hell, I might just stay in the Army my whole life!"

Riggs pulled off the side of the road, close to an old 3-wheeled rickshaw with an antique red Coca-Cola cooler strapped to the front.

"I guess we'll stop here for a soda. Chief needs to go shopping anyway."

Riggs and I stepped out of the truck just as the Chief was jumping out of the back. He started walking towards a ramshackle wooden hut not far away.

"Where's he going?" I asked.

"He'll be right back. That's what we call the 'drug store.' He's going in to buy him some weed."

"He's an MP, isn't he?"

"Yeah, but that don't matter here," Riggs answered.

We picked out two Cokes from the old red cooler, and Riggs paid for them. We went over to a small table that had once been a spool for cable or something. We sat down on two upside-down 5-gallon buckets that had been placed there for customers.

"Not a real fancy place, is it?" I said.

Riggs laughed.

I sipped on my soda and took in my surroundings. People in little conical hats were milling about all up and down both sides of the street. There was a flower stall nearby, and on occasion, I would catch of whiff of the different fragrances.

I noticed Riggs looking down the road. There was a car coming in the distance. It was a big car with huge free-standing chrome headlights leading the way, like a pair of giant eyeballs.

The car slowed as it entered the village. The big, black Citroën glistened in the midday sun. It came to a stop right behind our truck, close to the flower stand. The driver's door opened, and out stepped a snappy young man in a brown chauffeur's uniform. He turned around, opened the passenger door, and offered his hand. An elegantly dressed young woman in a large white-brimmed hat stepped out of the vehicle.

"Wow," I said. "I wonder who that is."

Citroën TA

"Probably some plantation's owner's daughter—or wife. There are still a bunch of rich French people who stayed behind after their forces got beat."

I stared at the young woman as she approached the flower stall. She was so formal, sophisticated, and seemed to radiate perfection. As she bent down to speak to the flower lady, I spied a large diamond necklace that sparkled around her neck. I had no idea that such opulence and elegance even existed in Vietnam.

"She must a métis," said Riggs.

"What? What's that?"

That's what they call the offspring of a foreigner and a Vietnamese national. She's probably half French, half Vietnamese."

I couldn't take my eyes off her. Her long, jet-black hair cascaded halfway down her back, and her large round piercing dark eyes demanded one's attention. Her high cheekbones and fine, delicate facial features added to her look of aristocracy. She seemed not to be wearing any makeup of any kind—it wasn't needed with her flawless complexion. She was a gentle flower: a delicate oriental flower the likes of which most men would never meet in a lifetime. She looked like all the pretty girls in the world all gathered up and rolled into one.

Riggs grabbed my arm. "C'mon, man. You can't stare at her for the rest of your life. We've got to go. The Chief's back."

The three of us climbed back into the truck and started down the road. I could still see the elegant woman in the truck mirror.

After most of an hour, we arrived at the base of an incline leading up a mountain range. "Almost there," announced Riggs. "This is the worst part of the whole trip. We've got to go six or seven kilometers up this mountain with three 180-degree switchbacks, one right after the other. They are a real challenge for the best of drivers, especially when covered in mist and fog. It's a real slow road, and the gooks like to hide out there and shoot at us. It looks like we've got us an escort today, though."

We were driving behind a South Korean armored personnel carrier and what appeared to be a gun truck going up the hill in front of that.

"You're the luckiest FNG in the world right now," said Riggs.

There's that term again.

"Why would that be?"

"Because this is the safest place in Vietnam, riding behind a Korean gun truck *and* an APC. The gooks are terrified of the Koreans. Nobody is going to bother us."

A US Army gun truck was coming from the other direction. Riggs gave them a wave as they passed.

U.S. guntruck (left) and South Korean APC and guntruck

"Those guys are with the 8th Transportation Group, up in Qui Nhon. They come down here all the time on regular patrol. We've got about three or four gun trucks that patrol this area all the time. They get shot up every few months. They don't last very long in this area."

"Wow, those are some pretty impressive trucks," I said.

"Yeah, they're heavily modified 2½ and 5-ton trucks. They patrol the roads at all hours of the day and night or provide escort for truck convoys carrying supplies to various camps. The US Army has between 300 and 400 of them fortified with armor plating and armed with .50-caliber machine guns. And let me tell you, they are capable of providing overwhelming firepower."

"I can imagine."

"The entire bed of those trucks is used for storing the ammo cans," Riggs told me. "Almost 10,000 rounds. The gunners have to stand on top of the cans the entire time. Crazy, huh?"

"Most of the gun trucks have four .50 cal's," added Riggs. "There's one up in Qui Nhon that has a 7.62 mm minigun mounted on it. I think it's named 'Lil' Respect' or something like that. They got the gun from a helicopter that had been shot down. It fires something like five thousand rounds a minute! I wonder where they store all *that* ammo. Doesn't much matter, though. Even with all that massive firepower, the trucks still get attacked all the time."

I had to admit that I did like having all the company. It gave me a sense of security. I took notice of how rocky the area was, a perfect hiding place for the enemy.

"What's that mean, anyway?" I asked, changing the subject.

"What?'

"FNG. I've heard it several times since arriving in-country."

Riggs threw his head back and bellowed. "Oh man, that means Fucking New Guy! That's what we call all of you new arrivals. You'll be an FNG until you've either been shot at or until another new guy arrives, whichever comes first."

Then Riggs just blathered on, explaining how only the misfits got sent to Vung Ro. He loved to talk fast and seemed an animated character, all wound up like a cobra ready to strike. He appeared to be a man of tireless energy, striking me as a thrill-seeker, someone addicted to risk—a real go-getter.

"...that way, they hide us away from the real Army until our year is up. Hell, we don't even have an officer up here. Our boss is a sergeant, a damn E-6. Military regulations and discipline are a thing of the past, man! We are the masters of our domain. Go figure that."

That statement got my attention. A worrisome thought occurred to me: maybe I was a misfit and didn't know it. Why else would I have been sent up here to an isolated post in the middle of the mountains?

We continued laboriously up through the steep switchbacks without incident. As soon as we reached the top of the mountain range, I could taste the salt in the air. I took a long, deep breath. It was cool, fresh, and clean—a pleasant and inviting odor—so different from the smell of the villages we had just come through.

Riggs turned off the main highway, and we began our slow mile-long descent down a narrow, winding, dirt road fringed with six-foot-tall elephant grass. One side of the road was a sheer drop-off down the cliff.

"What do you do if you meet somebody coming the other way," I asked.

"You pray," Riggs laughed. "You just have to drive over into the elephant grass and hope you don't hit a hidden boulder."

As we came to a clearing, Riggs pointed down to a sheltered cove.

"There's your new home for the next year!"

I peered through the windshield as the truck started down a steep hill. An oasis opened before me. I was stunned at the scene spread out below: a peaceful lagoon ringed on three sides by a chain of green mountains surrounding the bluest water I'd ever seen. Beyond the confines of the bay, a sky of Wedgewood blue sprinkled with wafts of white cotton-candy clouds floated gracefully across the horizon. The bay opened eastward towards the immense expanse of the magnificent South China Sea. Sunny white sand beaches, some decent-sized, some relatively small, dotted the shoreline around the bay. The water, however, no matter where you looked, was crystal blue. A gentle, delicate breeze blew in from the sea.

I did not expect anything like the peaceful and picturesque scene that greeted me. I had a difficult time appreciating that this was a war zone.

It could have been a scene from a travel brochure except for the two large landing ships nosed up to the beach, off-loading supplies. There was very little left of the natural lush foliage on the base side due to its having been sprayed many times with the defoliant Agent Orange, but it still could not rob the rest of the bay of its beauty. I was surprised that at least the hills across the bay were still green. The sapphire blue water was nice and clear, in stark contrast to the muddy, brown rivers of Saigon.

Vung Ro Bay (looking East)

"This is one of the most isolated places in 'Nam," said Riggs, "It's a vital deep-water port, though. Without Vung Ro, the airbase at Tuy Hoa and the Army camp at Phu Hiep wouldn't be able to be supplied. Everything comes in here:

fuel, ammo, napalm, bombs, artillery projectiles, food, PX supplies, you name it. It all comes in here and is either trucked north or taken up the coast by amphibious craft. The Viet Cong are always trying to blow up the fuel ships when they come in, so we've got to be extra careful when they're in port. We make sure we don't let any enemy sappers get near them. Concussion grenades are your best friend."

"What's a sapper?"

"Oh yeah, I keep forgetting that you're an FNG! A sapper is a Viet Cong swimmer, kind of like a commando."

We slowed just a little as Riggs drove through the checkpoint, which was nothing more than a bunker situated next to the road. Razor wire was stretched out in all directions, as far as I could see, to deter any intruders. I was fascinated by the way the wire glistened in the sunlight, each razor-sharp barb a sparkling invitation to pain and agony.

Perimeter Concertina Wire

I noticed a large white headstone situated on a hill nearby. "What's that?"

"Four Navy guys had their throats cut a couple of years ago. There was a lieutenant and three sailors. Gooks snuck into their hootch and killed them while they were sleeping. That monument was erected last year."

We drove on past a row of massive bunkers protecting the base. One bunker was situated high up on a hill. "That's Bunker 11 up there," Riggs pointed out. "It's been hit by two RPG's already, but the gooks can't take it down. Claymores surround them, and they've got two .50 caliber machine guns up there in addition to a Honeywell automatic grenade launcher. It's impregnable, man, totally impregnable."

The perimeter guard bunkers, Number 11 (on hill)
and Number 9 (right)

Riggs pulled up to a small complex of three or four buildings that sat right on the beach. Hopping out of the truck, I made my way around back to retrieve my duffel bag. Riggs came up and gestured off to the hills behind him. "It's a small base, man, only about three hundred or less in the whole place. We've got some stevedores up on the hill, then some bunker guards, a bunch of truck drivers, cooks, signal company people, and even some civilian contractors. Everybody is kind of scattered about. You'll learn your way around soon enough."

I looked around at the base behind me. It was nothing like the tropical scene that greeted me looking out into the bay. It looked more like a strip mine than an Army camp. Large heavily-armed guard bunkers, providing the illusion of safety, were spread out around the perimeter of the base. Nothing was growing anywhere—no grass, no plants, no trees, no shrubs—nothing.

Agent Orange had worked just fine.

Vung Ro Bay (looking West)

"That metal building up on the small knoll over there used to be a rather large motor pool," Riggs told me. "The company assigned there used to do a great job of keeping all our trucks and jeeps fixed, but they left, and now the building is home to a smaller motor pool. They don't fix nothing."

Riggs gave me the tour from where we stood.

"Below the old motor pool is the water purification plant, which is totally useless. You'll find that out really quick. To the right of that is the Vung Ro Bay Fire Station. To the left of the motor pool is the dunnage yard where all the lumber is kept."

"They get it all off the ships when they come in to unload," Riggs explained. "The wood is used to wedge everything in place down in the cargo holds."

Lumber Yard

"Over the hill," Riggs told me, "is a building housing the workers of RMK-BRJ, their equipment, and vehicles. It's a consortium of the four largest American construction companies. They are responsible for building much of Vietnam's infrastructure, such as dams, buildings, bridges, highways, piers, communications systems, etc. They have a small presence here in Vung Ro, but they're all over Vietnam. You'll see their orange vehicles all over the place. We don't get over there very often, though, and they never come down here. They kind of stay to themselves a lot. There are two other military outfits nearby; one is a South Korean White Horse Division unit. I told you about them on the way here. They're way up there," he said, pointing to the top of the ridgeline. "And way up above them, on the very top of Vung Ro Mountain, are several US Army Signal Companies. They handle Army communications with signal towers, microwaves, and all that stuff."

Grabbing my duffel bag, I followed Riggs inside and started getting introduced. There were fourteen men assigned to the Vung Ro PBR unit, though not all were present.

"There's a crew out on patrol," said Riggs. "They'll be back in later."

Everyone was sitting around in a small detached building known as the "dayroom." I looked around while being introduced. It was more like a small club with a bar, refrigerator, a couple of very old couches, and a few tables and chairs. It seemed like the place where everyone congregated. I shook hands with all who were present. They seemed like a good, cohesive group. They represented every corner of the United States: there was one from Tennessee, another from Kentucky. One guy said he was from Coos Bay, Oregon. I thought that was a strange name and made a mental note to ask about that one day soon. There was even a

Los Angeles surfer with bleached blond hair. He had a quiet, affirmative assurance about him as if he just knew that he was going to be somebody someday. His name was Kelly. He never wore a shirt around the compound and spent excessive time lying on the beach, working on his tan. When he wasn't doing that, he was in the dayroom lifting weights. Although I was never a witness to it, I suspected he also enjoyed looking at himself in the mirror.

I took an immediate liking to a kid from Pomeroy, Ohio, named Johnny Dees. Everyone was an E-4, except the NCOIC, an E-6, and the Maintenance guy, an SP-4 named Young. He had the difficult task of keeping the PBR's and Boston Whalers in running condition.

It was not all that difficult to pick out the ones who came from money. Young was a quiet, almost aloof, Spec-4 with a mustache who kept to himself a lot. I found out later that his father owned a dredging company in Florida. Another was the son of a mayor in Louisiana. Most, however, were just average young men like myself.

All in all, I was pleased with most of my new comrades. I had already pegged Riggs as the "go-to" guy. He was the one who could get anything done and, even though he was the same rank as all the rest of us, he appeared to be one of the leaders in the detachment. He seemed to enjoy the respect of all in the compound. I felt like I would fit in just fine here.

The one enigma was the Chief...

He just didn't make sense. He never joined in any of the activities, hardly ever left his room. He seemed much different from the rest of the group, like he was a part of us, but really not. He always seemed to be somewhere else. I had a tough time trying to figure him out. I learned later that he never frequented the dayroom or interacted with any crew, except for Riggs. He also had the strange habit of wearing sunglasses every minute of every day. I figured out pretty quickly that since he seemed to always be on drugs, he didn't want the NCOIC to see his eyes. I wondered if he slept in them.

Sign in front of PBR compound

Just then, the NCOIC came in and introduced himself. He was the guy in charge, an MP Sergeant First Class with a very pronounced German accent. I wanted to ask him how he got into the US Army but thought better of it. He showed me around the buildings. A Quonset hut anchored the complex. It had been re-configured with a center hallway and rooms on either side. Attached to one side of it was a wooden addition with sleeping areas. There were two or four to a room. Next to that was the shower—just a wooden stall with a big water tank up on the top. The NCOIC led me around the side of the building and down a wooden walkway, past ammunition storage Conex containers, a bunker, and then past the outhouse where he stopped to introduce me to the Vietnamese handyman, Papa-San.

"Papa-San!" the sergeant said. "New guy. New guy. FNG!" he smiled and pointed to me. "Papa-San's English isn't very good, but he gets the gist of things pretty easily."

Papa-San looked me up and down, smiled, and flipped me the finger.

Papa-San giving the American greeting

The NCOIC broke out in a fit of laughter. "Riggs taught him that—told him it was a common American greeting. He does it to everybody".

We continued walking past several Conex storage boxes lined up in a neat row.

"This is where we keep all our supplies. Everything from ammo to C-rations."

There was a young lady at a washtub. She looked up and smiled as we approached.

"This is Missy Soong," the sergeant said. "We use several local girls here to take care of the cleaning, washing, and ironing. None of them speak much English, though, so you'll have to use a lot of hand gestures."

I walked over and introduced myself. She just smiled.

Missy Soong

Our next stop was the beach where I spied the dock and... there it was—the mysterious PBR. I looked at it sitting there, bobbing up and down on the gentle sea swell. The back, or stern, was facing me, and a massive .50 caliber machine gun dominated the aft deck. The coxswains' position was covered with a canvas top. The boat looked fast. There were, in fact, two of them along with two Boston Whaler runabouts. The other crew had just come in from patrol.

PBR dock – Vung Ro Bay

We walked down to the water's edge and traversed a wooden gangway that was the ricketiest thing I had ever seen. Upon closer inspection, I realized that it was a series of short boards—many missing—that had been nailed at right angles to a telephone pole. One end of the pole was tied to the dock; the other end rested in beach sand. There were a couple of plywood sheets at the beginning, then four long boards, one of them broken in half. I wobbled a little as I crossed the thirty-foot span between the beach and floating dock, which was listing badly to one side. Upon reaching the floating dock, I had to walk at a fifteen to twenty-degree angle just to remain upright.

To what kind of an outfit had I been assigned?

"Be careful," the sergeant warned. "There are no plans to replace this dock anytime soon. It's just something we have to live with. It can be a bit challenging to get across sometimes, especially when we have to carry the .50-cals across."

He explained that, due to the salt air's corrosiveness, the .50s needed cleaning every time they were fired. That meant two guys removing them from the boats and struggling across the telephone pole, one at each end of the eighty-five-pound machine gun.

"Of course, if you unscrew the barrel and bring that over separately, you'll cut off 24 pounds. We have the cleaning tub up by the bunker. Most of the crews make it a two-man job, except for the Chief. He likes to carry his own guns by himself."

"You know, Sarge, I thought I would be assigned to a landing craft, carrying cargo up and down the rivers. I'm not trained on these boats. In fact, this is the first one I've ever seen."

A perplexed look came over the NCOIC's face. "That's very odd. You mean you didn't go to the PBR School at Mare Island?'

"No, sir. I've never heard of Mare Island."

"It's a US Navy training center in California. All of our boat crews are trained at the Navy PBR School there. Oh well, you're assigned to us—somehow. I'll put you on with one of the other guys for a day or two, so you can learn the ropes. And don't call me 'sir.' I work for a living."

A day or two? A day or two? How about a week or two!

I was intrigued by the heavily-armed PBR boats. The Sarge gave me the guided tour.

"They're thirty-two feet long with fiberglass hulls. You've got a gun tub in the bow that's fitted with twin electric-fire .50 calibers. You can take out boats, personnel, and even aircraft with these things. They fire at just over 450 rounds per minute at an effective range of 2,000 yards. You sit in the tub, and your left hand controls the crank to spin left and right. Your right hand manages the push button to fire the guns and adjust the angle of fire. There's an attached searchlight for night firing missions. We'll have someone show you how to set the head space and the timing. That's critical, or else they won't fire on fully automatic."

.50 caliber machine gun tub with searchlight

He led me back to the mid-ship's area.

"This is the coxswains flat, surrounded by armor plate, and down below is the radio room and storage. The engines are under these hatches we're standing on."

Pointing to an armored plate mounted between the engine hatches, he continued, "an M-60 machine gun is mounted on this side, and over here is a Honeywell grenade launcher. It fires 40mm high explosive fragmentation grenades, 250 rounds per minute, at ranges up to 300 yards or so."

On the stern was a standard .50-caliber machine gun mounted on a tripod. "This is a manual-fire .50 cal."

Then the sergeant opened a hatch and showed me the twin V-6 Detroit Diesels. Another hatch exposed the Jacuzzi water jet drives.

"What! No propellers or rudders?" I asked, somewhat amazed. I had been trained on nothing else.

"Nope. These jet drives enable the boat to travel in shallow water without clogging up the props with weeds or other crap. At high speed, it gets up on a plane, and all you need is 9 inches of water depth."

I was fascinated by this new craft. I was looking forward to operating one.

"Our mission here is to protect the harbor and make sure visiting ships are safe. We get all kinds of vessels in here, ranging from landing craft to oil tankers. We get cargo ships more than anything, though. They bring in all the bombs and stuff for the airbase. Oil tankers present a very critical situation, though. They moor to four anchor buoys on the other side of DeLong Pier and hook up to a 4-inch underwater multi-fuel pipeline that pumps 36,000 gallons an hour up and over the mountains to a petroleum storage point four miles inland. From there, it goes through a 16-

mile pipeline to Tuy Hoa. It's crucial that no sappers ever get near those ships!"

We started back down the rickety dock. "Oh, one more thing... we have a stringent rule here. Never, ever get out of the boat—not for any reason. Not for any reason whatsoever." His words were emphatic, and I looked at him for further explanation.

"It's a good way to get surprised by the Viet Cong and get yourself killed," he continued. "If you're in the boat, not only do you have all these weapons at your disposal, but you can get away if need be."

458th PBR compound, dock, and helipad

I met the remainder of the crew and then went to settle into my room. As a coxswain, I was entitled to my own room. It was in the corner of the Quonset hut and had a small window hinged at the top. It was small, with just a single steel bed, a footlocker, and a steel locker in the corner. I was happy to at least have a decent bed with an actual mattress and a pillow. I had heard that a lot of soldiers in Vietnam had to sleep on folding canvas cots. I would not have liked that.

This is it, I thought—my new home for the next year.

My first task was to pin up the short-timer's calendar I had acquired down in Saigon. Many of the calendars started when someone had 90 or 120 days left in-country, someone told me. Mine started at 365 days. That's how I wanted it. I would mark off a little box with a number in it every day. I wanted to know exactly how many days I had left at any given moment.

I liked to move into clean quarters, so I set about pulling the locker, bed, and footlocker away from the walls to sweep behind them. My mother would have liked that.

I slid my footlocker out about a foot or two from the wall. A photo lay on the floor behind it. I picked it up and dusted it off. It was a photo of a pretty red-headed girl in a bright yellow sundress. Her face was full of freckles, but she wore them well. Her eyes reminded me of a hand-held sparkler on the 4th of July.

I looked at the photo for the longest time, not quite sure what to do with it. It didn't seem right to just dispose of it— she was somebody's girl. And besides... she was too pretty to throw away.

After much thought, I taped the photo to the inside of my locker door. "Well, Mystery Girl, it's just you and me now," I whispered. I looked at her several times a week but showed no one. She hung there for a year. I don't know why.

That night I lay on the bunk in my new room for the first time. I could hear the sea through my open window, gently lapping at the soft sandy beach just a few feet away. The night air was cool and crisp, a soft, gentle breeze rolling across the water.

Curious, I got up out of my bunk and gazed out the window. The moonlight sent a soft glow splashing across the calm waters of the bay. In the dark sky above, stars glittered brightly as if cast about with random abandon. It was almost surreal.

Not too bad... I thought... Not too bad.

.

I was startled awake in the middle of my first night in Vung Ro Bay by a massive concentration of machine gun fire. I raced outside, expecting to find everyone on the base engaged in an enormous firefight. I found nothing. Everyone was still asleep, like nothing had happened. Suddenly, it was quiet again. I looked around for a few minutes and found no one stirring, so I went back to bed. At breakfast the next morning, I mentioned the incident to Riggs.

"Oh, don't worry about that," he said. "It happens all the time. It's called a 'mad minute.' It's a tactic where all the bunker guards open up with machine guns at the same time and saturate the surrounding area with as much firepower as possible. It's kind of a brute force approach to combating an invisible enemy, I guess."

At first, it was very annoying, but I soon learned to sleep through it. Even in sleep, I could tell the difference between the 'mad minutes' and incoming. When there was incoming, I was up and running before I was even awake; such was my natural survival instinct to get under cover of the bunker next door.

.

The sound of diesel engines being revved up to a high RPM woke me. I glanced out of my little window. Dawn had slipped away to make room for the morning sun. A fresh, gentle sea breeze swept across my face like a splash of cold water. The bay was flat calm, quiet, and peaceful. There did not seem to be a war going on.

The noise grew louder; a huge amphibious craft, a 60-ton BARC, was inching its way up the concrete boat ramp next door. The 9-foot-tall tires slipped a little on the wet concrete surface even though a 220-hp diesel engine drove each wheel. They had come down from Tuy Hoa to pick up supplies delivered by a cargo ship the previous day. A front-end loader was being driven onto the deck of a landing craft just next to that.

L to R: A Landing Craft Utility (LCU) and a BARC

I had an immediate nightmare visualization of being assigned to a landing craft known as an LCU, or worse, a BARC. Neither one could go much over ten mph, and that's if the wind was with them. I shuddered at the thought of spending a year in Vietnam on one of them. What a boring job that must be. Then I came to my senses. The PBRs were going to be so much better. I was going to enjoy this place, providing I didn't get shot. I had yet to come under any enemy fire. I had never seen death and had no desire to get a taste of it. Some of the others exuded a bravado of sorts, probably lying to themselves about their own bravery and fearlessness. I just wanted to live—to get back home to my family.

I missed the smell of a truck stop.

I had to admit that the small size of the base at Vung Ro Bay made me nervous. Very, very nervous.

Now fully awake, I removed the stick holding my window open, lowered and closed it, and made my way outside to the outdoor shower, hoping to get in ahead of most of the others.

A few were stirring, but most were still in bed.

Riggs was standing outside the dayroom as I came out. "Going for a shower?" he asked. "Let me show you something that may save your life."

I opened the wooden door to the stall and stepped in. Riggs was right behind me.

"You have to use this little plastic soap dish to turn the water on and off. We've got a water heater out back—I stole it from the Air Force—but it must be wired wrong, 'cause every once in a while, this faucet will shock the hell out of you. It doesn't do it all the time, just when you're least expecting it. Just put this soap dish over the handle to turn the water on and off, and you'll be fine. Oh, and don't mind the smell. All the water around here has JP-4 jet fuel in it."

Riggs went back to the dayroom, and I wet myself down, then soaped up, and turned the water off—a Navy shower. Riggs told me that the tank up on top of the shower held enough water for all, but conservation was still necessary. Once completely lathered, hair included, I reached to turn on the water again. Nothing. I made sure the soap dish was positioned correctly, turned the faucet off and on a couple of times, hoping it was stuck. Still nothing.

I just stood there, wondering what to do, soap all over my body. Then I heard bursts of laughter coming from the dayroom. Riggs came out and walked over to the shower, still laughing.

"I guess we'll let you finish your shower." He said as he went around the back. A minute later, I had water again.

PBR Compound (ladder leading up to water tank)

The crew thought the shower episode was hilarious, of course. I learned that the valve on the tank could be accessed by sneaking around the back of the shower and climbing a ladder, unseen by any shower occupant.

I had received my first FNG initiation.

A couple of months later, the heating element in the water heater must have burned out, or else it shorted itself out. Anyway, it quit working at all. For the rest of my time in Vietnam, I had cold showers.

It was my first full day in Vung Ro Bay. I joined the pranksters heading up the hill to the mess hall, where breakfast was in full swing.

"How did you like your shower, FNG?' Kelly asked, laughing.

"Oh, just fine, thanks," I replied.

The small dining hall was packed. We had to stand in line outside for a few minutes. Two Vietnamese mess boys were washing and drying plates at the door. One of the bunker guards was throwing a Bowie knife at the side of the wooden building. Between throws, he would spit out a well-used wad of chewing tobacco. Tacked to the mess hall wall was an 8x10 photo of the U.S. Commander in Vietnam, General William Westmoreland. The knife thrower had ripped it with care from the pages of a magazine. The picture had holes all over it but none on the General's face.

"Hey! You with the new green fatigues! FNG! Wanna stand up against this here wall, and I'll throw a few knives around your head?"

"Don't mind him," came a voice from behind me. "He's always looking for suckers."

I just smiled and kept moving with the line.

Thunk!... Thunk!... Thunk!

He was pretty good with it, though. It turned out he was from Kentucky, the mountains of Appalachia, and had been throwing knives all his life. One of the others mentioned that he had dreams of joining the circus after his tour in Vietnam—as a knife thrower, of course.

The mess hall had been built from scrap lumber. Every piece of wood had once been a piece of dunnage; lumber used to secure cargo in the merchant ship's holds. When the cargo was unloaded, so was the dunnage. It somehow found its way up to the small hill where members of the 119th Transportation Company had built the mess hall during their off-duty hours. It wasn't a fancy building, but it served its purpose very well. The tables and benches that crowded the room were built from scrap lumber. Even the counters that were used to serve the food were scrap lumber. I was pleased that we at least had metal trays to eat from. Some of the windows had screens over them. Others looked as though the screens had been missing for quite some time. The building looked like it had seen better days even though it wasn't more than five years old. The weather just took its toll. A rusty water tank stood out back.

Vung Ro Bay Mess Hall

The line whittled its way down. Edging my way inside, I grabbed a tray and some silverware. I selected powdered eggs, bacon, potatoes, and jello for breakfast.

One bite was all it took. "Yuk. This stuff tastes like diesel fuel!"

"Get used to it, man," Riggs said from behind me. "Everything that's cooked using water—powdered eggs, potatoes, jello, anything—has the flavor of jet fuel. We've got a filtration plant down the hill there. It's a trailer-mounted unit that they say is supposed to purify the water, but it never does a very good job of getting the fuel odor out. You can filter the water 'til the cows come home, but you still ain't gonna get the JP-4 taste out of it."

"You've gotta be kidding me. Why is that? That's absurd!"

"Well, the tankers that come into the bay pump fuel through an above-ground pipeline that runs across one end of the water basin then across the mountains to the Air Force Base. The Viet Cong shoots holes in the pipe and sometimes blows it up. Anyway, sooner or later, jet fuel drains into the Vung Ro water supply. It's not a lot, just enough to leave a thin film on the surface, but unfortunately, the taste is always there. It's supposed to be safe to drink, but I have my doubts about that. Anyway, it makes a good excuse to drink more beer!"

I ran into the cook just as I was leaving the mess hall. "Hey," I said. "I'm not trying to be a complainer, but is this the best the food is going to get around here?"

"Probably is," he answered. "I have a lot of trouble getting anything decent. All the good stuff goes to the Air Force base at Tuy Hoa and the Army camp at Phu Hiep. We're such a small, isolated base, so all we get are the scraps: the stuff that nobody else wants."

The cook seemed like he tried his best to make things appetizing, but there was only so much he could do.

At least we had C-Rations, the good old standard military boxed meals.

4. All Aboard!

The NCOIC had paired me for training with Bill McCall, a guy from upstate New York. He had been in-country only two months longer than me, but two months is a lifetime in Vietnam. He was no longer an FNG. McCall took me down to the dock and showed me around the boat again, as the Sarge had done the day before. After going over a mental checklist, McCall went down below decks and emerged with two boxes of C-Rations.

"What's your pleasure—Spaghetti or Spaghetti?" Removing the main course cans from the boxes, he opened an engine room hatch and placed the cans on the exhaust manifold. "They'll be piping hot by lunchtime. By the way, you need to learn this now. The trick to getting the good C-Rations is to sneak up to the Conex at night just after a new shipment arrives. We go through them and bring all the good ones down to the boat. We like Spaghetti, Meatballs & Beans, or Meat Loaf the best. Leave the Ham and Lima Beans behind."

Stepping into a small armor-plated area, McCall pulled down a swivel driver's seat. "This is called the coxswain's flat," he said. "This will be your home for the next year."

McCall pushed the starter buttons, and the engines roared to life, the deep-throated big diesels reverberating in the early morning stillness. The two MPs untied the bow, spring, and stern lines and coiled them on the deck. McCall gently turned the wheel towards the pier, put the starboard engine slow ahead and the port engine slow astern and maneuvered the boat away from the dock. After clearing the dock, he 'shifted rudder' and eased the boat's two throttle controls forward as the craft slipped across the calm, still water, headed out into the open bay. The waves were minimal, the result of a gentle sea breeze blowing from the east. The water glistened in the early morning sun like thousands of giant diamonds gently bobbing on the surface. It was a perfect day to be on the water. McCall increased the speed until the bow dropped down on step, and a wide swath of white water shot out from the sides. The little boat was flying across the water at twenty-eight knots.

"That's it," he yelled over the growl of the big diesels. "Wide open! Pretty cool, huh?"

I was standing next to McCall in the coxswain's flat, sporting a stupid grin. *This is going to be a lot of fun!* I thought. *So much better than a landing craft.*

The boat was barreling across the bay; the two MPs were standing in the stern talking. An engineer should have been aboard to round out the crew, but he was absent that day for some reason.

"You might want to find something to grab hold of for just a minute," McCall said. "I've got a special maneuver to teach you."

I reached up and held onto the overhead canvas shelter.

"No, grab something better than that."

I wrapped both hands over the top of the steel armor plate surrounding the coxswain's flat just in time.

The boat was traveling at full speed—the throttles were wide open. McCall reached over, grabbed the starboard throttle lever, and yanked it all the way back while simultaneously spinning the wheel hard right.

PBR Doing 180° Flip

The boat did a 180° flip in its own length. It was just incredible. One moment it was barreling across the water, headed for the ocean, then before I even realized it, it had flipped around and was going the other direction. My stomach went to my throat. I had a hard time keeping my balance. I was scared half to death but had never experienced anything as thrilling or exciting in my life.

That was it. I was hooked.

The boat skimmed along, the big diesels screaming, heading for the opposite coastline across the bay. Suddenly, McCall yelled out, "Contact!" and the crew scrambled to their weapons. One MP ran up to the bow and jumped into the forward gun tub. There was an unmistakable metal-on-metal sound as he racked the .50 caliber's bolts and chambered a round in each. The other MP took a position on the aft machine gun, spreading his feet just a little to absorb any possible recoil. He, too, slammed a round into the chamber. In that brief moment, I saw more live firepower made ready to fight than I had ever before experienced.

"Well, Hebert, it's time to get your feet wet," exclaimed McCall. "We've got to check out this sampan. You may as well give it a shot."

River Patrol Boat at full speed

I looked at the vessel off our bow. It was a wooden craft with a slightly raised bow and stern and propelled by oar power. A tiny cabin, not even big enough to provide shelter, occupied the center of the boat.

"What are they doing out here?"

"Who knows? They might be fishermen, although that looks unlikely—no nets. They're probably merchants of some type. See what they have on board."

He took the time to explain everything that I needed to do: what contraband to look for and how a proper ID should look.

The PBR took several more minutes to reach the sampan with four men on board. Pulling up alongside, McCall brought the PBR to a gentle stop. I picked up a coiled line and got ready to throw one end of it to one of the men aboard the sampan.

"No!" yelled McCall. "Never tie yourself up to a sampan. If the shit hits the fan, we're stuck."

I threw the line down on the deck next to the midships cleat. One of the MPs handed me an M-16 rifle and motioned me over the side. I grabbed the weapon and looked at McCall.

He gave me a short, crisp salute and smiled.

I looked at the group of four young Vietnamese standing on the deck of their sampan. I studied each of their faces, searching for some sign of friendliness. Each just glared at me. None were smiling. They all looked like Viet Cong to me.

Hebert inspecting suspected Viet Cong sampan

I was not happy. I could feel my hands starting to get clammy. I reached up and wiped away the few beads of sweat beginning to form on my forehead. I hoped the Vietnamese didn't notice.

"Y'know, McCall, Sarge told me to never, ever get out of the boat, no matter what."

"Go on!" yelled McCall. "Get on down there. Sarge isn't here."

Dressed only in a white T-shirt and fatigue pants, I grabbed the gunwale and hoisted myself over onto the sampan. I had never been in a sampan before, much less one with four Viet Cong who might like to kill me. I tried to act like I was in control of the situation, even though I was scared to death. My fingers fumbled to find the trigger on my M-16.

I heard McCall demand, "Can Cuoc." The Vietnamese produced scruffy-looking identification cards that appeared well-used. I stepped over to the PBR hull and handed the cards to McCall, who returned them after much scrutiny.

"Check under the deck boards," he yelled.

I lifted every deck board I could find and then checked inside the small cabin. All was clear. The four Vietnamese had no merchandise on board, no weapons, no fish, no nothing.

We sent the sampan on its way.

"I don't know if I want to do that very often," I said to McCall. "That was kind of scary."

"You'll get used to it. They were probably all VC anyway. We just can't prove it."

McCall eased the boat up to one of the enormous anchor buoys used to moor the fuel tankers. They were a convenient place to tie up the PBRs when there were no tankers in port, mainly because they were well away from the eyes of the NCOIC. The MP climbed out of the gun tub and tied the bow line to the buoy's large steel mooring ring.

McCall shut the engines down and announced, "Lunchtime!"

Retrieving the cans of spaghetti from the engine manifold, he threw one to me. One of the MPs went below and came back up with the rest of the C-rations. They each had a box. The MPs seemed displeased with their selection, one of them mumbling something derogatory about Ham and Lima Beans. I proceeded to work on opening my can with one of the Army's never-fail implements: the P-38 can opener, a small, folding, hand-held device that could be attached to one's dog tags.

The Spaghetti and Meatballs wasn't all that bad. I finished off my lunch with a small can of pound cake and a chocolate cocoa disc, which was the worst excuse for a candy bar ever. Since I didn't smoke, I gave the little four-pack of cigarettes to one of the MPs.

"I keep telling you guys," McCall chided, "You've got to go through those C-Ration cases before you bring them on the boat. You never listen to me."

"It wouldn't matter anyway," one replied. "All the Spaghetti is always gone."

•

I settled in and learned how to operate the PBRs in no time at all. I was amazed at the difference between this craft and the landing craft upon which I was trained. Of World War II fame, landing craft were used in Vietnam to run up on a beach, load cargo or personnel, and transport them somewhere. The PBR, in contrast, was like a sports car. Its maneuverability and speed was just a hoot—plain and simple.

"We like to think our crews work like a well-oiled machine," said McCall. "Each crewman knows what is expected of him, and they are all comfortable in knowing how each other would react in a time of crisis."

"That's good to know," I answered.

"The workday here is divided into two shifts of twelve hours on duty, twelve hours off. The day shifts start at 0600, but that's not set in stone. Some days we start at 0700, some days at 0800, whatever. It all depends on how much partying we do the night before," he laughed.

■

"What's that up on that mountain?" I asked McCall on our second day of training.

"That's called Da Bia," he replied. "It's a giant boulder up on the mountaintop that we suspect is a Viet Cong hideout. There's a large cave up there that the Koreans search on occasion. We call it 'finger rock.' F-4 Phantoms from Tuy Hoa fly by regularly and drop a few bombs or make some strafing runs. You'll see them quite a bit."

Vung Ro Bay with Da Bia in distance

There were two PBRs at Vung Ro, on occasion three, but it was customary to use only one per shift unless we were under attack. A crew of four staffed each boat: the coxswain, an engineer, and two Military Police.

The crews alternated shifts every week, and the night shift soon became my favorite. I enjoyed drifting around out in the bay and watching the sun set slowly over the mountains, sending streaks of light beaming towards the sky. It never lasted very long, though, and we would then start up the engines and get underway. After a cursory sweep of the harbor and bays for an hour or two, we would motor over and tie up to one of the mooring buoys used to secure the fuel ships. With the arrival of nightfall, the mountains surrounding the bay faded away into a gray mist, then got darker and darker until they were completely invisible. The four mooring buoys were located on the far side of the DeLong pier and hidden from the view of the NCOIC. Tying up to these mooring buoys at night made me uneasy, though. I always worried about enemy swimmers sneaking up on us and blowing up the boat. We would sleep in two-hour watches, a couple on the engine hatches, one in the hammock below deck, and one on guard listening for signs of enemy activity. The quiet calm of the sea combined with the eerie stillness of a pitch-black night always instilled a sense of fear.

It made you pay close attention to the sounds of the night.

When scheduled for the day shift, things were a bit different. We still tied up to the buoys a lot, but the daylight afforded greater recreational opportunities. From my vantage point on the big steel buoy, I could keep an eye on the entire harbor—the entrance, the opposite shore, the bays, and the ocean. It was quite relaxing and safe out on the buoy, offering a picturesque view of the harbor. It would take a pretty good sniper to knock us off at such a distance.

We could see all of the perimeter bunkers from our vantage point out in the bay. The huge wooden guard towers spread along the boundary of our base. The guards were always black, shadowy figures lurking about, moving silently from one side to the other, looking for Viet Cong or anything out of the ordinary.

I remember one particular day when I was lounging out on the buoy as if it was my own private deck. The sun was at its peak, but it wasn't unbearable.

It was a beautiful day in Vung Ro Bay.

I took a sip of my Hamm's beer. I spied my fatigue shirt that I had dropped beside my chair a bit earlier. The Sea Tigers patch on the pocket caught my eye. The motto read *Ever Vigilant*. I thought about that for a moment... it was a good motto and I felt proud to be assigned to that unit.

Ever Vigilant on the Mooring Buoy

I turned the radio up a little louder, took another sip of beer, picked up my book, and stretched out in my lawn chair... Ever Vigilant.

It didn't take me very long to realize that the group of young soldiers I had just become a member of was more like a band of brothers than a formal, disciplined Army unit. Nobody used anyone's real name. Everybody had a nickname; some predicated on a particular talent, some complimentary, some not. Others were shortened or reduced to initials. My nickname became the same as the number of my boat: 'Three Two.'

•

"Three-two!" yelled Kelly, the MP. "Get your boots on. We're going to town."

It was my first trip off of the base since my arrival several weeks prior. "OK, give me a second. I'll be right there."

I ran to my room and threw my boots on. I would lace them up in the truck. Going to the Air Force base for the day was an adventure I was determined not to miss. I ran outside and jumped in the back of Old Betsy with several others. Riggs was at the wheel.

I held on for dear life—an uncontrollable grin plastered across my face—as Riggs careened down the mountain road. He was driving like there was no tomorrow. Boulders rose out of sight up the mountain; on the other side, a cliff fell to the valley below. Guardrails were non-existent. If you went off the road, you were dead.

I glanced over the side of the old truck—the wind whipping my hair into a tangled mess and causing my eyes to tear up. The tires were spitting rocks up and shooting them off the side of the cliff. I watched them for an instant as they disappeared over the edge, dropped out of sight, and fell several hundred meters to the bottom. My ears were filled with the sound of angry tires screeching, stretching, and groaning at every turn. My body jarred with every bump in the pot-hole-filled road. Riggs was downshifting with abandon as the truck sped down the mountain. My nostrils filled with the scent of baked-on dirt and oil wafting up from the hot engine. The worn-out little 6-cylinder engine sounded as if it would explode into a million pieces at any moment.

"Damn it, Riggs!" yelled Kelly. "You always drive like a madman. Can you slow it down just a little? I'd like to get home in one piece, not in a damn body bag."

Riggs offered a quick grin as he glanced back at me through the canvas window of the cab. "No problem. We have to slow down anyway; we're almost at the crossing."

Armored MP jeep & blown-up bridge on Highway QL-1

We were approaching the remnants of a blown-up bridge on Highway QL-1. Nothing was left but a big, gaping hole in the earth littered with dirt and rocks.

"This is the fourth time the Viet Cong have blown this bridge up since I've been here," said Riggs. "It seems to take the Army Engineers longer to rebuild it each time."

"Maybe they've gotten smart and just given up," said Kelly. "The Viet Cong are pretty good at taking out bridges."

A single-lane dirt crossing had been constructed in haste next to where the bridge used to be. An armored Military Police jeep fitted with an M-60 machine gun was almost across, coming from the other direction. Riggs waved as they passed by. Once across the bridge, Riggs took off again. The road down the mountain featured several tight turns and three 180-degree switchbacks that required vehicles to slow to less than ten mph, making them perfect targets for Viet Cong snipers. To Riggs, though, the switchbacks were but a challenge.

"This is making me a bit nervous," I yelled to Riggs through the canvas window of the cab.

"Calm down, man! I'll get you to the base safely."

I sat back down on the bench seat and closed my eyes for a moment. Even though we had crested the peak of the ridge, I could still smell the pungent aroma of the sea blowing in from across the top of the mountain range.

The tremendous *KAPOW!* got my immediate attention. The old truck started to swerve violently back and forth across the narrow highway. Riggs was fighting the wheel for control. A million thoughts whizzed through my head. What the hell was happening? Had something hit us—an RPG, a mortar, a land mine? My training automatically kicked in as I jumped up, chambered a round in my M-16, and began to fire on fully automatic, spraying the mountainous hillside and kicking up little puffs of dirt. Some rounds were ricocheting off the rocks and taking off into the bright blue sky. I tried in vain to spot an enemy—anybody with a gun. I was firing wildly, shooting at anything and everything. Spent shells were flying all over the back of the truck bed.

"What the hell are you doing?" yelled Riggs, still fighting the wheel and trying to regain control. Kelly was in the front passenger seat, laughing like an idiot.

"Front tire blew out. Hang on and stop that damn shooting!"

Gradually, Riggs regained control and brought the truck to a safe stop, pulling off the road next to a boulder-laden cliff.

I breathed a sigh of relief. "I thought we'd been hit."

Riggs laughed. "You're scared to death of getting killed, aren't you? Relax, man. You're in good hands."

The three of us jumped out and surveyed the damage. The balding front tire had seen better days. There was not much left of it. The other tires were the same.

"What are we doing driving on these?" I asked. "They're all bald as can be."

"We're the quintessential bastard unit, man," replied Riggs. "Nobody knows we exist, and if they did, they wouldn't care. Even headquarters tries to ignore us—look at the crap they give us to get around in. Old Betsy should have been in the junkyard years ago. Hell, we were lucky to get *these* tires."

I looked around and realized that we had already traversed all three switchbacks coming down Vung Ro

Mountain without me even realizing it. I could see the lake in the distance.

Highway QL-1 near bottom of Vung Ro Mountain,
Lake Hâo Son in the distance.

"We've got to hurry up," said Riggs. "This is a favorite spot for the Viet Cong to stage ambushes. Hebert, let's you and me take up firing positions. You take the front, and I'll watch the back. Kelly, since you think everything is so damn funny, why don't you change the tire?"

"How's the spare look?" I yelled to Kelly as I took up my position in front of the truck.

"Guess!" came the reply.

Kelly was almost finished changing the tire when the distinct diesel whistle of a 5-ton truck caught our attention. Looking downhill, we watched as a massive US Army gun truck came rolling around the bend. The truck slowed as it approached us. The name *Eve of Destruction* was plastered across both sides in giant white letters and .50-caliber machine guns bristled from various areas of the back.

"What's the problem?" yelled one of the gunners, perched in the corner of the bed.

"Just a flat," answered Riggs. "We've almost got it done now. Where are you guys headed?"

"We're just going up the mountain to sit along the road for a bit. Got to keep Charlie awake!"

"Well, you guys do a good job of it. We're heading down to Tuy Hoa for the day."

"Good luck to you guys," shouted the gunner as the big truck increased RPM's and crept up the hill.

∎

"All right, came the shout from Kelly. "Where to first?"

We had arrived at Tuy Hoa Air Force Base. I was excited about my first visit to the base. Riggs gunned the old truck past the Security Police gate guard, not concerned about stopping. That was one of the nice things about being assigned to the river boat company—they were attached to a Military Police unit. Old Betsy was emblazoned with a *Military Police* decal beneath the windshield, plainly visible to the guards. We could do just about anything we wanted to. We opted to visit the snack bar first.

"This is going to be quite an adventure," I said to Riggs. "I can't wait to get a real hamburger."

Riggs whipped the truck into a spot right outside the door, right next to a big deuce and a half. We all bounded out, grabbed our M-16's and put our .45 caliber pistol belts on. We adjusted our berets—to make the optimal impression—and filed into the snack bar. Riggs was the last one in and let the screen door slam shut behind him as he entered—not unlike walking into a saloon at high noon. Everyone in the room turned to look.

"Let's get this table in the corner," said Kelly.

There were quite a few Air Force personnel and a bunch of soldiers from the Army camp at Phu Hiep, seven kilometers to the south. A few were staring at us. We removed our black berets, placed them on the table to hold our spot, and made our way to the counter.

"What you rikee?" asked the Vietnamese lady, wiping her hands on the front of her apron.

"I think we'll all have burgers and fries," answered Riggs. "... and milkshakes."

"Mikshakee machiney brokee."

"OK, then just burgers, fries, and cokes."

"You rikee chee?"

"Yes, ma'am," smiled Riggs. "Cheese on all of them."

We returned to our tables with cokes in hand and waited for our orders.

An Air Force master sergeant in a flight line uniform was seated at the next table and studied us with great interest. "What's with the black berets?" he asked. "Who are you guys?"

"We're from a gunboat unit down in Vung Ro Bay," answered Riggs. "It's about an hour's drive over the mountains to the south. We get to wear the beret's 'cause we were crazy enough to volunteer to do what we do, except for this guy," he said, pointing at me. "They give us fancy hats to keep us pacified!"

The sergeant laughed, slid his chair back, grabbed a bright orange flight line vest, and threw it over his left shoulder. "Well, you guys enjoy your day, and have a safe trip back."

"Thanks, Sarge," said Riggs.

He paused to scoop up a few items of trash from his table and headed for the garbage cans. "And don't try to steal anything! We know how you Army types are."

Riggs laughed and got up as the cook called our order. Riggs insisted on paying for our meals.

After enjoying my first hamburger in months, we decided to visit the PX, located several buildings away.

"You guys go ahead," said Riggs. "I've got an errand to run. I'll meet you there soon."

An hour later, Riggs showed up, and we all went to the EM Club for a few beers. After a couple of hours, we left the club for the ride back to Vung Ro. Riggs waved to the gate guard on the way out of the base—a brand-new tire mounted to the side of the truck.

"Where did you get that?" I asked.

"I just drove around the base until I spotted an Air Force truck off by itself next to a hanger. There wasn't anybody around, so I sort of borrowed a tire." He smiled.

5. What's in a Name?

I was assigned as the operator of PBR J-7832. One of the perks of being appointed as a coxswain in Vietnam was the right to name your boat. There had been another PBR, a relief boat, at Vung Ro Bay for a short time called *Death Dealers*. That did not sit very well with me. I thought it was a terrible name. Not wanting to follow along in that vein, I thought long and hard about a name for PBR-32.

The other boat in Vung Ro, the PBR-29, was assigned to McCall. It was also unnamed. The two of us sat around quite a bit, drinking beer, trying to come up with names for our boats.

"I've got it!" McCall exclaimed one afternoon in the dayroom, tilting his beer can to drain the last drop out. "I'm naming my boat after my favorite comic book hero: *Captain America*."

I thought that was an excellent name for a boat and tried several times to talk McCall out of it since I wanted it for my boat. But he was unwavering. He had one of the stevedores in camp design and paint the name on wooden plaques that adorned the sides of the boat, right below the words "Military Police." The sign was all done in red, white, and blue Stars & Stripes lettering. I thought it was marvelous.

I struggled to come up with a decent name. Several had come to mind, but I dismissed them. One day, I read a magazine article about a movie featuring Ringo Starr, Peter

Sellers, and Raquel Welch. It was about a ship, *The Magic Christian*, staffed by a bevy of beautiful women.

Aha, I envisaged a boat full of beautiful women. What could be better than that? There's my name! And so, the next day, I set about designing and painting my signs, and voila! *Magic Christian* was born.

PBR-32 Signboard

Our Quonset hut was metal. During the day, it just absorbed the heat and kept it through the night. Even with my window open and the constant sea breeze blowing, it was still hot. My tiny little desk fan only seemed to blow hot air my way. Some nights I just lay there in a puddle of sweat.

I remember one night not being able to sleep; I got up, went outside, and walked along the beach. The night sky was the darkest I had ever seen. I looked up into the heavens. Vung Ro Bay was only 13° North Latitude, close to the equator, making the stars and formations seem extraordinarily large, especially the Southern Cross, which was clearly visible at that time of year.

The boat dock was off to my left. The lone PBR tied up there glistened in the moonlight as it rode up and down on the gentle incoming sea swell. I gazed out into the sea, surveyed the base, the beach, the bunkers, and the buildings. The stars were exceptionally bright, and all was quiet, peaceful, and inviting. It was a beautiful night in Vung Ro Bay.

.

We were fortunate in our billet. There were never any officers around. The head honcho was an E-6, just a notch above our own rating, and we all pretty much lived the good life. Most of us had little refrigerators in our rooms, generally stocked with our favorite beverage: Olympia beer.

In the room next to me was Bill McCall. He had a much larger refrigerator than I did. I don't remember how or why, but he did. It was always very, very well-stocked.

I remember entering the hallway to our hootch one afternoon. McCall had just returned from patrol, and he was fuming!

"What's the matter?" I asked.

"My damn beer is disappearing faster than I can drink it! Some son of a bitch is stealing from me."

Not knowing who the culprit was, McCall set about doing some detective work. After a few days, he had determined that it was none other than our NCOIC, the boss himself.

"What are you going to do?" I asked. "We're both E-4's, and he's an E-6".

A smile came over McCall's lips. "No problem. I've got a plan."

A few days later, everyone seemed to be off doing other things. The hootches were empty. McCall and I took a hand grenade from the Conex storage and gently transported it out behind the hootch. He unscrewed the firing mechanism, set the grenade aside, and pulled the pin on the handle, blowing the fuse. Then we put the firing mechanism back together and screwed it back into the grenade. McCall and I took it to his room, secured it to the second shelf of his refrigerator, then ran a small line from the grenade pin to the inside of the door. If someone opened the door, the pin would fly off and scare the hell out of them, but nobody would be injured.

Coming back from patrol the next day, McCall discovered that the pin was out of the grenade.

Strangely enough, that was the last time any beer went missing.

I walked into the dayroom just as Riggs was telling the story of the dead sapper to a couple of the bunker guards who had stopped by for a beer. I walked up to the bar, plopped down 10 cents to purchase a beer, and then went back to the table to listen to the rest of the tale.

"... so, this Army helicopter was on a routine patrol above Vung Ro Bay and spotted a floating object in the water off Echo Beach. He turned around, landed at the helipad, and reported the sighting to our MP desk. They radioed the PBR that was out on patrol, and they went to check it out."

When was this?" I asked.

"Long before you got here, man," Riggs answered.

"Anyway, The PBR pulled up alongside what they thought was just a floating log. They had been dropping concussion grenades around the pier earlier that morning. As they pulled up to this log, they discovered that it was a body! Not only that, but it had explosives tied to it. The body was face down with a box the size of a C-ration case floating next to it. The sapper was even wearing a crude scuba-type diving suit with a mouthpiece and a long stiff plastic tube so he could breathe underwater."

"How did they know there was an enemy swimmer in the area?" asked an FNG.

"They didn't," answered Riggs. "The PBR crews regularly tossed concussion grenades, each packed with one pound of TNT, into the water during patrol activities. You throw them close to the ships and piers. Hopefully, the grenades are enough to deter enemy swimmers. We call them 'sappers.' Anyway, in this case, it worked."

Riggs stopped and chugged down half his beer. "The condition of the body indicated that it had probably been in the water for at least three or four days. One of the MPs on the boat stripped down to his skivvies and dove into the bay. He had to get close to the floating body without endangering the other men on the PBR. He discovered that the diver had a Russian-made floating sea mine concealed in the box. It was secured to the diver with a rope. The MP swam back to the PBR, retrieved a knife, and cut the line. Then they lassoed both the body and the box, tied them to the stern of the boat, and towed them to shore. Once on land, they covered the body with a tarp and called an Explosive Ordnance Disposal unit from Phu Hiep. EOD said the diver had about 75 pounds of explosives in the mine. They disarmed the mine and blew it up on the beach. The body of the Viet Cong diver was turned over to local authorities."

Jimmy Dees was fascinated by the event. "When did you say that happened, Riggs?"

"Oh, sometime early in '69. Around February, I think." Riggs answered.

I had already been in-country for more than twenty days. Nothing very exciting or dangerous had transpired so far. I hadn't even been shot at yet. I remember always being worried about that. Would my courage show up when I needed it? When you're getting shot at, there's not much time to think; there's only the reflex of survival.

You either have it, or you don't.

I enjoyed these infrequent sessions in the dayroom. Riggs was on his second tour in Vietnam and had a ton of stories to recount. Like any uninitiated newcomer, I was anxious for a bit of action. Nothing really serious, just a dead Viet Cong or two would suffice.

6. FNG Graduation

It was one of those nights that you just never forget, no matter how old you become. I had been in-country for precisely three weeks. I had the day off and had just come from a leisurely evening on the beach, catching the last rays of the sun before they disappeared behind the mountains to the west side of the bay. My euphoria at being stationed in paradise ended abruptly on a calm, peaceful Friday night. I had just crawled into my rack and was just about to doze off when all hell broke loose. The quiet still of the night was shattered by the sound of concentrated automatic weapons fire. Loud explosions surrounded me. They were slow at first, then intensified rapidly. I could hear yelling and screaming coming from all corners of the compound.

I jumped up out of bed, opened my locker, and noticed the photo. "Well, Mystery Girl, this is it. Wish me luck!"

I hurried to put on some clothes, pulled my combat boots on, and started to lace them. My hands were shaking.

I couldn't get my boots tied.

I tore the boots off my feet, grabbed my flip-flops, threw on a flak jacket, a helmet, and ran to the arms room to pick up my M-16.

I ran outside. Soldiers were running everywhere. This was definitely not a 'mad minute.' The entire base was gripped in confusion and pandemonium as mortars rained down upon us with fury. Machine gun fire rang out as bunker guards woke up, sobered up, or came down from their high.

The Viet Cong had launched a massive attack from all directions. We had been surrounded on three sides and never knew it. I hoped we weren't getting over-run. It was my very first firefight.

Was it going to be my last?

My heart was pounding. The sound of my own breathing amplified in my head. It was all I could hear. I took a deep breath, trying to keep my composure. Everything was moving so fast! I felt a sweat break out on my forehead. There would be no more wondering, no more worrying about my abilities in combat—the day was here! There was so much happening that I had a hard time trying to think. I was scared to death. The sounds of war petrified me, yet it was also the most incredible adrenaline rush I'd ever had.

Massive explosions continued to echo throughout the bay. The night sky lit up like a fireworks show. I looked up as I ran in the direction of our bunker. There were illumination flares everywhere, chasing the darkness away. White ones, red ones, then more white ones. The night air was smoky and hazy, thick with the odor of burning phosphorus.

There's something magical about a flare going off. First, the initial "pop" of the canister being fired, then a shrill "shriek" as it screams skyward, and finally a louder "pop" followed by an explosion of light. The sky filled with little parachutes drifting down from the heavens, swaying from side to side in the calm night air, the eerie glow casting alternating shadows wherever the bright light penetrated.

Looking out into the bay, I could see the two PBRs firing along the hillside. They each had all three big guns blazing away along with an occasional M-79 grenade. I smiled for a moment. There is nothing—absolutely nothing—like the raucous thunder of a .50-caliber machine gun.

Something landed near me with a small *thud*. I looked down. A hand grenade lay in the dirt not ten feet away.

"Three two—Mike. In here!"

It was Riggs, yelling from the safety of the bunker next to our hootches. There were a half-dozen others with him, including the NCOIC. It wasn't an elaborate bunker but nonetheless offered relative shelter.

I took a flying leap inside, almost knocking Riggs to the ground.

"Down!" I yelled, "Grenade!"

Everyone scrambled for the cover of the sandbags. Those unlucky enough to have neglected to grab their helmets just clamped their hands on top of their heads. We waited for the blast. And waited... and waited... and waited.

Nothing happened.

Vung Ro Bay bunker, grenade in foreground
(Photo re-staged following day)

"Damn," I yelled to Riggs. "It's a dud! How lucky is that?"

We all raised our heads above the sandbags and stared at the little grenade lying peacefully in the sand.

"Cover me," I screamed to Kelly. "I'm goin' for it."

"No, Three-two. That's a stupid idea," one of the others yelled as I was halfway out of the bunker.

I hurried to the grenade, grabbed it up, and ran back to the safety of the bunker, holding the grenade up for all to see.

"Hebert," the NCOIC said. "Sometimes, you're pretty dumb."

"Yeah, I know. A girl back home used to tell me that all the time."

"Get that damn thing out of here, you idiot!" screamed Riggs.

"OK, OK." I stepped back outside the bunker and threw the grenade as hard as I could down towards the beach, halfway expecting it to go off. It still didn't explode. "Don't forget, when this is over, that grenade is mine."

"OK, what do we do now?" asked Kelly.

"Find something to shoot at," howled Riggs.

"He's really a cowboy," whispered Kelly. "He was just born in the wrong century."

I took up a position next to Riggs, hoisted my weapon to my shoulder, peered out of the slit in the bunker wall, and let loose with a barrage of automatic M-16 fire. I could feel my heart racing, the adrenaline building. The danger and imminent threat of death made me feel more alert than I had ever been in my life. Every shadow, every slight noise, got my immediate attention.

There was too much going on to be afraid.

"Make sure you can see something to shoot at, Three-two!" the NCOIC shouted. "Try to save your ammo. We don't know how long this is going to last."

I stopped firing. "I can't see any enemy anywhere. It's pitch black out there. By the time I hear a bullet, the muzzle flash is already gone."

"Then just lay low and sit tight." Riggs hollered.

Bullets were flying everywhere. Tracers and ricochets filled my vision. I thanked God every time I heard a gunshot, though. They say that you never hear the bullet that kills you, and I sure as hell didn't want to find out if that was true or not.

I thought a lot about death. I didn't know if it scared me or not. It was such a strange and incomprehensible idea to me. In one moment, I could be alive, feeling, seeing, touching, hurting, loving, and in the next moment—if a bullet found its mark—I could be dead. I would cease to exist. I just wouldn't be there any longer. Death... it was such a strange concept.

I hugged the inside wall of the bunker, hoping the closer I got, the safer I would be. I could feel the sandbags digging into me. Every so often, I raised my head and fired off a few rounds, just to let the enemy know I was still there. Once in a while, I felt the deadly *thud-thud-thud* of enemy AK-47 rounds slamming into the outer sandbag wall, thuds that seemed to pass through my entire body. I stopped hugging the sandbags and backed off a little bit, just in case...

It all came to an end about two hours later. The attack just stopped abruptly. It was as though they had all just given up and gone home.

The excitement and danger of combat had arrived, and I had finally gotten the action I had wished. I realized how close I had just come to getting shot, maybe killed. My left leg started to twitch uncontrollably.

I didn't wish for action anymore.

"OK, it looks like that's it for the night," announced Riggs. "Let's get over to the dayroom. I need a beer."

Those of us in the bunker slung our M-16's over our shoulders, slipped our helmets back on our heads a little bit, and trudged off towards the compound, combat veterans, all!

"I'll meet you guys in the dayroom," I yelled and ran off down to the beach to retrieve my war souvenir.

When I got to the dayroom, several bunker guards and other Vung Ro Bay personnel were already in place, chugging down some much-needed comfort.

Riggs had gathered up a small group at the corner table and was going over the battle in detail.

As I walked in the door, I heard him say, "... and he picked it up—still live, mind you—and walked right into the bunker with it, calm as could be."

I became the hero of the night. Everyone wanted to see the grenade. I don't know who thought I was stupid or thought I was brave, but they all wanted to see it.

I showed it to all but allowed no one to touch it.

The stories continued well into the night. After about the third or fourth beer, the realization struck me that I had come through the battle with flying colors. I was now a real soldier.

I wasn't an FNG anymore.

The next day I took my hand grenade apart and cleaned all of the explosives out of it. Today it resides proudly on a shelf in my living room.

·

The Viet Cong attacked the base frequently but not fervently. The little gook bastards were invisible and seemed to enjoy harassing us invaders with machine-gun fire, mortars, and rocket-propelled grenades, most of the time on Friday nights. I had become used to the regular Friday night

Viet Cong attacks and gave up trying to sleep on those nights. I just stayed up and waited for the event to occur, waiting for the mortar rounds to start dropping like magic from the dark night sky.

It was standard operating procedure to get the second PBR underway when the VC attacked. I started the first few weeks wearing a flak vest, steel helmet, fatigues, and boots but soon gave in to wearing just a pair of shorts and a T-shirt. It took too much time to get dressed, the flak vest felt like a ton of bricks on my shoulders, and the steel helmet got in the way on the boat. We were authorized to wear deck shoes while on the boats anyway, so I just wore them all the time.

One particular Friday night, the mortars started coming in. I ran down to the pier, being the first to arrive at the boat. I jumped in, started the engines, and anxiously waited for the rest of the crew to arrive.

It was one of the darkest nights I can remember. There seemed to be a lot of those in Vietnam.

Suddenly, I heard several very rapid *splat-splat-splat* noises right behind me, just off the stern. It was a sound that I was unfamiliar with and, for a moment, did not recognize.

For an instant, I thought it might be fish jumping.

Then it came again: *splat-splat-splat*. I looked around just in time to see several areas of water splashing up, not two feet away from the transom... bullets. Whoever was shooting was 'walking' the rounds ever closer to my boat—and me!

Frantically, I dove out from behind the protective armor of the coxswain's flat and ran up to the bow. I untied the line and threw it off onto the dock, then ran back to the stern. As I let the stern line go, several more rounds hit the water, this time only inches from the boat. I had to remind myself to keep calm and remain focused. Keep breathing evenly.

Just then, two of the MPs came running down the pier and jumped on the back deck.

"Grab something and hold on," I yelled. "We're outta here."

I hurried back to the controls, maneuvered the bow away from the dock, rammed the throttles forward, and sped away. The MP on the stern was already firing the .50-caliber in the direction of the incoming rounds. The other MP was making his way to the forward gun tub.

As we cleared the pier, I saw my engineer running down towards the dock, waving his arms.

"One more coming!" the MP on the stern gun yelled.

"There's no way I'm going back to that dock! We'll just have to operate one man short."

I ran the boat up to speed. The waves beneath us became but a blur; the sea turned black as we sped across, stirring up frothy water and illuminating the plankton behind us.

PBR 32 "Magic Christian" after a battle mission

The source of the incoming rounds seemed to be the perimeter of our base, so the MPs concentrated firing their big .50-caliber machine guns on that area. The powerful searchlight mounted to the side of the bow gun tub swung back and forth across the shoreline, lighting up the night sky. We shot at everything. We shot rocks, we shot trees, we shot dirt, you name it.

Hell, we even shot each other...

I was nervous about shooting that close to our own bunkers, but it had to be done. Red tracer rounds spat out into the night.

Captain America arrived on the scene from patrol across the bay and brought its full firepower to bear on the shore near where we were firing. I radioed McCall and suggested they move a bit further down the cove and fire in that area.

.50-caliber tracer rounds during Vung Ro Bay firefight

McCall agreed and moved his boat in that direction. The MPs were spraying gunfire all over the hillside. The red tracer rounds—every fifth bullet—fanned out across the black night. It looked like some kid had taken a red crayon and drawn lines across the sky.

If the engineer had made it aboard, he would be manning the Honeywell grenade launcher. It was my favorite toy, capable of spitting out 40mm grenades at a rate of up to 250 per minute. I was itching to operate it, but there was no way I could leave the helm. I maneuvered the PBR a bit closer to shore, thankful that I wasn't being fired upon anymore. I was right between the gunners, one in the front and one in the back. All I could hear was the constant rhythmic booming of the three .50 calibers. The concussion of their combined blasts thumped my whole body and caused my ears to ring in pain. One gun would stop for a little bit on occasion, then start back up. Even though they had a firing rate of over 500 rounds per minute, the MPs frequently paused to avoid burning out the barrels through overheating. I knew that this was going to be a barrel-replacement night anyway. I wondered why the MPs even bothered giving the guns a rest, then realized that they still had to try to conserve the barrels as much as possible. Overheating a barrel in the middle of a firefight was not a good idea. It would severely diminish the effective range of the bullets.

The *Captain America* was spitting out bullets and tracers all over the darkened hillside. On the *Magic Christian,* we were making a slow approach to the end of the Vung Ro perimeter.

I looked up just in time to see one of the tracer rounds from the *Captain America* hit a boulder on shore and then ricochet directly into one of the guard tower bunkers.

My radio crackled. "Whoa! Did you see that?" It was McCall. He had witnessed the tracer incident also.

The battle lasted for another half hour or so. Tracers and rockets created a scene that was somehow disturbingly beautiful.

The next day McCall and I were having breakfast in the mess hall and overheard others talking about the bunker guard who had been grazed in the head the night before by a .50-caliber round that had pierced his helmet. While attempting to make his way down the bunker tower ladder, the guard, dazed and bloodied, became dizzy from his wound, slipped, and fell the last six or seven feet to the ground. He made his way to the medic shack, where his head injury was treated and bandaged. It was a close call.

He was later awarded the Purple Heart for being wounded in combat.

A week later, I was out on a night patrol with Kelly, and an FNG MP. It was a typical hot, quiet night as we motored around the bay at a slow speed.

"What the hell is that?" yelled Kelly.

I looked towards where he was pointing, up along the mountainside leading to the Korean Compound. The Koreans had trip flares placed at intervals going up the hillside. They were being set off in succession, one by one. We watched as flare after flare was detonated, starting with lower levels, then progressing up the hill.

"That's seven of them so far," Kelly said. "Gooks wouldn't be that stupid. It must be a tiger or a water buffalo setting them off."

The Koreans let loose with a couple of Claymores, then started with small arms fire, shooting down the mountainside.

We happened to be drifting right in the area where the bullets were landing.

"32. Get us the hell outta here, now!" Kelly yelled.

I pushed both throttles full ahead and sped away from the incoming rounds.

"Damn. That was too close for comfort," I said. "I guess they couldn't tell that we were down here."

"Well, we don't use running lights at night, so nobody's going to see us anyway."

∙

McCall quickly became a good friend. We were both coxswains and enjoyed trying to outdo one another. McCall was already ahead with the boat-naming thing.

I enjoyed listening to him recount the story of how he managed to acquire his handlebar mustache and managed to keep it in the United States Army. The subject came up frequently whenever an FNG arrived at the base and became curious about it.

Before reporting for duty in Vietnam, McCall had been selected to serve aboard River Patrol Boats. He was sent to the Naval Inshore Operations Training School at Mare Island, California, an Army E-4 attending a Navy school.

At that time, Admiral Elmo Zumwalt, Commander of Naval Forces, had issued a decree that all naval personnel would be permitted to grow facial hair: mustaches and beards. The Army did not allow that, and MP units were the fussiest.

"I somehow became friends with a Navy Lieutenant," McCall told me. "We were discussing mustaches, and I told him how much I wanted a handlebar. He told me that I should use this golden opportunity to grow one. I told him that they weren't permitted in the Army."

Several days later, McCall again met up with the Lieutenant, who had come up with a brilliant plan.

"Look," he said, "It's a regulation in the service that you have to look like your ID card. Why don't you grow your mustache while you're here with the Navy, lose your ID card, and then go get another one showing you with a handlebar mustache?"

McCall was very skeptical but went ahead with the idea anyway. He grew a nice handlebar mustache, 'lost' his ID card, and went to the Navy facility to replace it. No one there batted an eye, of course, and his new ID was issued.

Arriving in Vietnam, he was challenged on multiple occasions by Army officers who didn't like his appearance. Each time he produced his military ID card showing him with a handlebar mustache.

McCall proudly sported his handlebar mustache for the duration of his tour in Vietnam.

7. The Sampan

Early one morning, we were out on patrol, running at a slow speed near the mouth of the bay. We were running with only a three-man crew; Riggs, Kelly, and me. I don't remember why we didn't have an engineer. Sometimes, if there was some maintenance to be done onshore, the engineer would stay behind. We were bored, bored to death.

"Hey! There's a sampan out there, past Hon Nua Island," said Riggs. "Let's go check it out."

"I don't know," I replied. "That's out of our patrol area for sure."

"What the hell, Three-two. It's something to do."

"Yeah, it's better than sitting out here doing nothing," added Kelly. "Besides, they might be VC. Who knows?"

"Yeah, I guess so," I said and increased speed as I guided the patrol boat in their direction.

A few minutes later, two Vietnamese fishermen looked up in terror as our dark green river patrol boat came screaming up at them, skimming across the top of the water. I pulled up alongside, not making any effort to slow down to cut the effect of my wake. The little sampan rocked violently to one side, then the other, almost knocking the two men into the water.

Kelly, the MP on the stern .50 caliber machine gun, yelled at them to produce their identification. "Con Cuoc! Con Cuoc!" Riggs stood on the port engine hatch, M-16 at the ready.

The two fishermen just stood there. One was but a mere youth, the other well into his 80's. The younger one reached in his pocket, produced his ID, and handed it to Riggs.

Papa-San in his sampan

"Con Cuoc! Con Cuoc!" Kelly yelled again to the old man, but he just grinned, showing the two or three teeth he had left.

"Con Cuoc!" Kelly yelled again.

The old man stared at him and suddenly became very sullen and started to yell at us in Vietnamese. None of us could understand a word.

"Never mind," I yelled to Kelly. "We'll just take them on in."

"Sounds good to me," he replied. "Sounds like the old man's kind of pissed off anyway."

"Rig a towing bridle between the two aft cleats, then tie the sampan to it with a bowline."

Kelly grabbed a line and jumped into the sampan. He pushed past the two men and went to the bow. "There's no cleats on this thing!"

"Well, just wrap the line around the bowsprit, then. That should hold." I answered.

We brought the two fishermen aboard the PBR for the trip back to Vung Ro Bay. They both went to the stern, the young boy squatting near the starboard muffler. Riggs stood guard over them with a 12-gauge shotgun. The old man was furious, yelling and shaking his fists at us.

I put the PBR in gear and slowly took up the slack on the tow line. I ran the boat up to a slow cruising speed, and we settled in for the trip back to the bay. We had traveled a little more than half the distance to the bay when the old man just blew his fuse. He was screaming, yelling, and probably cursing at us.

The sampan sinking beneath the water

About this time, I had decided that I was over this nonsense. I reached for the throttles and shoved them both forward. I looked around just in time to see the two fishermen fall to the deck. The old man got up just in time to witness his sampan split apart in the middle and sink to the bottom of the bay. The shock and disbelief was evident on his face as he turned back around and glared at me. His eyes hated me.

He just stood there. He never said another word.

Arriving at the PBR dock in Vung Ro Bay, the two fishermen were turned over to a waiting South Vietnamese Police Officer who interrogated them at great length before determining that they were just a harmless old fisherman and his grandson. They were released and walked five kilometers back to their village.

To this day, I still regret my foolish and youthful actions of so many years ago. In a fit of anger, I more than likely had deprived the poor old fisherman of his only livelihood.

8. The Spec Five

About a month after my arrival, we welcomed our new maintenance NCO. As usual, Riggs and the Chief drove to Tuy Hoa to pick him up at the Air Force Base.

A bunch of us were sitting in the dayroom when the NCOIC brought him in for introductions.

"This is our new maintenance guy," he announced. "Lee Beckman."

We all raised our beers in a welcome cheer, and someone popped open a can of Olympia and handed it to Beckman.

"Where you from, Lee?" I asked.

"Well," he answered, staring into his can. "I'm from all over, I guess. My last residence was Ohio State University."

"What was your major?" one of the others asked. Beckman was our one and only college boy.

"Animal Science," he answered with a smile.

"What?" said Riggs. "How the hell did you get sent to us? We're a boat outfit. Ain't no cows anywhere near here."

Beckman managed a short laugh then explained, "I got drafted during my summer break from school. I only had one more quarter to go. Anyway, at the Induction Center, I found out that two-thirds of the recruits were going to the Marines, so I signed up for a third year and got to pick a school. They gave me this big book to go through, and I picked out Amphibian Engineer since it taught diesel engine stuff. After my tour here, I intend to go into Ranch Management, so diesel experience will be a big plus."

"So, that still doesn't explain how you got sent to PBRs," said Riggs.

"Yeah, I know," Beckman said. "Sorry. I was trained on LARC's at Fort Story, then sent to Fort Eustis for leadership school. They made us all Spec 5's right out of school. When I got here, they assigned me to the 458th PBRs. I had no idea what was going on. My first week in-country, I was running up and down the Saigon River escorting freighters and tankers. That was a real eye-opener! I'll never forget all those little shanty houses built out over the river with a hole in the floor for a toilet. At low tide, we'd watch the crap pile up, and by high tide, it was all gone. I don't know where it all went, but I'll never swim in that river!"

Laughter engulfed the room, and we opened more beers. We were going to like this new guy.

That night, Beckman's first night in Vung Ro Bay, would stay with him forever. He had just returned from the shower and was settling in for a much-needed sleep when sniper fire began pounding the metal walls of the Quonset hut.

Ping-Ping-Ping!

Mortars began to rain down upon our base. The attack lasted over an hour. The bunker guards opened up with everything they had, spraying the surrounding hillsides with fire from their .50 calibers, M-60s, M-16s, and M-79 grenades.

During the attack, Beckman huddled with the rest of us in the bunker next to our hootch. "I think I'd rather have stayed in Saigon. This is way too much excitement for me."

On his second night, the VC gave us a rest, which didn't last long. For the next two weeks, it was sniper fire or mortar attacks two nights out of three.

"You know,' Beckman said to me one morning at breakfast, "I did the math on this attack stuff. There are 365 days in a year, and we're getting hit two-thirds of the time, so that's 240 days we'll have to dodge bullets or mortars. We'll be lucky as hell to make it out of here alive."

"Yeah, it might be a better idea to just move into the bunker," I joked.

Luckily, soon after that, the incoming slowed down to the standard rate of every week or so.

∎

A small group of us were walking back down the hill from the mess hall. Lunch, as usual, was miserable.

We heard banging sounds, then more banging, and then someone yelled, "You damn piece of shit!"

Riggs was trying to start Old Betsy for our weekly run to the Army camp at Phu Hiep. It was the only way we had to get our mail.

After more tinkering, hammering, banging, and clanging, Riggs had had enough. "That's it," he yelled. "I can't get this damn thing going. We'll have to go get the mail the old-fashioned way."

A loud groan arose from the group.

"What's he talking about?" Beckman whispered to me.

"You'll see soon enough." This was Beckman's first time going *to town*. "Just wait here and have a beer. We'll be going soon."

"One of you run over to the Delong Pier and see when a truck's leaving for Tuy Hoa," Riggs said. "Tell them to stop by here on their way out."

Not thirty minutes later, a big 5-ton truck rumbled to a stop in front of our dayroom. "All right. All aboard if you're going," yelled Riggs.

"Come on, Lee," I said. "This is how they used to have to go get the mail before either of us got here—in the back of a bomb truck."

Several of us climbed into the back of the 5-ton. Pallets full of 500-pound bombs were occupying most of the space.

There were four bombs to a bundle, each weighing in at one ton. There were four pallets on this truck. We squeezed by a couple of pallets and made our way to the front of the bed. Riggs banged on the roof, and the driver put the truck in gear and eased away from our compound.

"Man, I don't like this at all," said Beckman, a look of grave concern on his face. "None of this stuff is even secured."

"Oh, don't worry," Riggs said. "It gets worse."

Less than thirty minutes later, Beckman was praying for his life to be spared. The bomb truck had reached the switchbacks going down the mountain and was in the process of a sharp left turn.

"Watch out!" Riggs yelled as one of the bomb pallets started to shift. "Move out of the way when one of those things comes towards you, or you'll get crushed to death."

"Why don't they tie those things down?" asked Beckman.

"Don't know," answered Riggs. "There's only a foot or so between them, and they can't go anywhere in the back of this 5-ton. They normally don't have passengers, either."

We danced our way around the shifting bomb pallets for several more miles, anticipating the next turn, until the road leveled out in the valley below.

"Whew!" exclaimed Beckman. "I'm glad that's over. I hope we can get that old truck running again."

Several hours later, we hitched a ride back to the bay with the same bomb truck. This time it was empty. Beckman had a smile on his face all the way back.

The trip back to the bay was uneventful until reaching Deo Ca Pass. The huge bomb truck came to a crawl near one of the switchbacks. A group of South Koreans was strung out up the side of the mountain. They were throwing something to each other.

"What's going on?" Beckman asked.

"Koreans," answered Riggs. "Looks like they've killed themselves some Viet Cong."

Beckman watched in awe and disgust. The Koreans were throwing bodies. They would lob one out into space from high up on the mountain; it would fall 30 or 40 feet down, then another group would pick it up and throw it again, further down. They seemed to be enjoying themselves. This went on until the body reached the road below, where two soldiers loaded it onto a truck.

We rode the bomb trucks to get our mail for the next several weeks. Old Betsy needed a new fuel pump, and one was on order. We would get it soon, the NCOIC told us.

Beckman, for some odd reason, chose to ride the bomb trucks whenever he could. I think he enjoyed the challenge.

"Man, you shoulda rode with me today," he told me one time. "The bombs were chasing us all over the back of the truck because they didn't have a full load. Those damn things were sliding all over the place! The pallets were sliding around the bed, corner to corner, front to back. We had to be on our toes the whole time to make sure we moved out of the way in time to avoid getting squashed to death."

.

A couple of weeks later, we were all sitting around in the dayroom when the NCOIC walked in. "Riggs! Get the truck ready and go to Tuy Hoa. You'll be picking up our company XO. He's coming in from Saigon for an inspection.

"What the hell," barked Riggs. "He must be a new guy. Officers *never* come up here. They know better."

"Why is that?" I asked, confused.

"They're afraid of what they'll find. Then they'll have a mountain of paperwork to bog them down for days, even weeks. What you don't know won't hurt you," he said with a laugh.

"And somebody change the water in that water cooler." the NCOIC said, pointing to the beat-up old cooler in the corner of the dayroom.

"Won't do any good, Sarge," said Riggs. "The yucky color is from the JP-4 that's in it. We can change that water all day long—won't do any good."

"Well, cover the damn thing up, then. I don't want the XO to see it. That thing has already caused me enough headache."

A week earlier, an Army Chaplain from Qui Nhon had given a Sunday service. Unfortunately, the Chaplain held it in our dayroom, and he was none too pleased with the brackish-looking water in the cooler. After returning to Qui Nhon, he called the Commanding Officer of the 127th M.P. Company and complained about it. The CO thought that one of us had complained to the Chaplain about it, so he called our NCOIC and read him the riot act. The water cooler never changed.

∎

He was a tall young lieutenant with an easy-going manner and a long, unpronounceable name of Polish origin. We showed him around the compound, then led him down to the dock where he bravely traversed the rickety walkway leading to the boats. When he got onto the dock, he almost slipped due to the angle of the decking.

"This is a bit odd," he said.

"Yes, LT, but it's all we got," Beckman said.

I was already aboard my boat and motioned for the lieutenant to step aboard. The first thing I noticed about him was the size of his boots. He must have worn a size 12 easily.

He and Beckman settled into conversation on the stern while I maneuvered away from the pier and headed out into the bay. Beckman explained our fire zones, various types of missions, and then we returned to the dock just in time for dinner.

"Come with me, Lieutenant," Beckman said. "The mess hall is right up the hill over there."

It was one of those typical days when everything was all screwed up. I was looking for a tray when Beckman and the LT showed up. The scent of fried chicken permeated the air.

Outside the mess hall door were two 55-gallon garbage cans full of cold soapy water stacked to overflowing with dirty trays, a sure-fire case of dysentery waiting to happen. There were no clean trays anywhere. The Vietnamese staff that usually cleaned them had all gone home early for some reason unknown to us. Beckman and I were embarrassed to have our visiting XO witness this fiasco. Somehow, we swished some soapy water around and managed to make our trays halfway clean enough.

We entered the mess hall and started down the line. We were limited to only three chicken wings and instant mashed potatoes that tasted like jet fuel, jello that tasted like jet fuel, and Kool-Aid that tasted like jet fuel. For dessert, we had pineapple.

Fat Cook—that's what they called him—was standing at the end of the line, hands clasped in front of his apron. He was beaming from ear to ear like he was waiting for a medal or something. He couldn't cook worth a damn, but he was nonetheless proud of his creations. He had attended a culinary school for a year before being drafted—or, so he told everyone. He just couldn't seem to remember which one.

"More damn pineapple!" Beckman told the XO. "For the past four months straight, we've had pineapple: chunks, rings, and crushed. For breakfast, lunch, and dinner."

"Is this what you guys have to eat?" he asked.

"Hell, LT, you're here on a good night. At least you can tell what the chicken wings are! We usually have some kind of mystery meat in gravy that tastes like jet fuel."

Two days later, a pallet of C-rations arrived from Qui Nhon suspended under a Huey helicopter. The chopper hovered over the helipad for a moment, set the pallet down in the sand nearby, released the cable, and flew off.

Our entire detachment ran out and surrounded the pallet, determined to keep any others stationed in the bay from getting any. Let them eat chicken wings. It's a sad day when C-rations are more desirable than real food.

■

One morning Beckman was fuming.

"What wrong, Lee?" I asked. We were on our way to breakfast. More eggs with JP-4.

"Well, me and that new MP who's rooming with me just can't seem to find all the holes in our roof. Every time it rains, we find a few, then when the rains stop, we'll take some tar up there and patch what we can. Just when we think we've got it fixed, a thunderstorm hits, and we get leaks all over the place! Last night Hickens was in his top bunk, and drips hit him in the face, so he started complaining. I told him to suck it up and quit bitching. Well, guess what he did?"

"What?"

"He jumped down off his bunk, grabbed his mattress, and found a spot on the other side of the room.

"So, what's wrong with that?" I asked.

"Well, with no mattress on top, the raindrops started hitting me in my face. We finally had to move the whole set of bunks."

■

Beckman came running into the dayroom, beaming from ear to ear, his hand holding a small package. "Look what I got in the mail today! My girlfriend sent it."

"A pack of watermelon seeds," I said. "What are you going to do with those? There's no good dirt around here anywhere."

"Ha!" said Beckman. "You just wait. You'll see."

That afternoon he scoured the area around our compound, looking for just the right home for a watermelon patch. Finding a suitable location close to his room, he planted the seeds.

"You can't grow watermelons in beach sand!" the NCOIC said upon learning of Beckman's plans.

"Sarge, I'm a farm boy. I can grow anything."

"Yeah, well... we'll see about that."

Sure enough, the next thing you knew, tiny watermelons started to spout. Beckman was very secretive about his methods, making sure to tend the plants when nobody was around. The melons grew and grew — right there in the beach sand that everyone scoffed about.

"I have to hand it to you, Beckman," the NCOIC told him one afternoon. "I never thought watermelons would grow in beach sand. This is a new one for me."

"Well, Sarge," Beckman answered. "Just wait until they're ripe."

The melons kept growing, getting bigger and bigger. It didn't take very long for word to spread around the camp that the PBR guys had fresh watermelons. As they ripened, we sliced them up and served them in the dayroom whenever there were no soldiers from any of the other units around. There just wasn't enough to share.

Beckman caught me as I was going into the shower one morning. "Three-two, we've got a major problem."

"What's the matter, Lee? One of the boats broke down?"

"Worse than that. Someone snuck into the patch last night and stole two of my best melons!"

Well, that was a crime that could not be tolerated. From that point on, Beckman put a volunteer crew on night watch to guard over the patch.

"Lee, how's that going to work?' I asked. "The crews are already working 12-hours shifts. Now they'll have to work more?"

"It's only a 2-hour shift," he answered. "And it's voluntary. Of course, anyone who doesn't volunteer probably won't be getting any melon."

"Hmm... OK, well, we'll see how that goes."

All went well for the next week or so. Volunteers stood guard over the melon patch with M-16's at the ready, just in case some of the stevedores down the road got hungry. Then early one morning, after the guard had left and before the rest of the crew got moving about, a fire somehow broke out in the middle of the patch.

I was sitting in the dayroom listening to some music on the tape player when Beckman burst in. "Hebert! Grab an extinguisher. You've got to come with me. Hurry!"

I ran outside and saw our beloved watermelon patch ablaze. I put the fire out after several minutes, but the damage had been done. We knew it had to have been set, probably by the stevedores or maybe even the bunker guards, but nothing could be proven.

Disheartened, Beckman came up to me and said, "That's it for me, anyway. The watermelons aren't worth the effort, what with having to guard them and all. And some of the guys are starting to complain about watching them at night. I'm tired of all the bunker guards and stevedores trying to steal them. Besides, they're way too much work. I need a break."

Hebert dousing the watermelon patch fire

■

"Three-two, give me a hand with this damn thing, will you?" Beckman yelled as he nosed one of our Boston Whalers up to the beach.

I had just walked out the back door of the radio room and was heading to the pink outhouse. I walked over to where he had landed.

"What's the problem?" I asked.

"This damn Whaler's acting up again. It won't stay running at all. I hate these Johnson outboards."

The two of us pulled the small craft up higher on the sand.

"Try not to scratch the paint," I said. "Dees and I spent a lot of time getting this thing so pretty."

"Yeah, Beckman laughed. "Every time some officer shows up, we have to hide that boat so they don't see the red stripe. I don't think that's exactly regulation!"

"Yeah, but I'll bet it's the prettiest Boston Whaler in the US Army."

Boston Whaler w/40 HP Johnson

We managed to drag the craft well above the high tide line so that it wouldn't float away, and Beckman unscrewed the handles that secured the engine. I helped him lift the outboard off the transom and laid it in the sand.

"Wait here for a second." He said and scurried off to the maintenance shed just a few yards away. He returned a minute later with a stretcher.

"What's that for?" I asked.

"We've got to get this thing up to the shed, and it's too damn heavy to carry. This will work just fine."

And it did. We got the engine to the maintenance shed, and both of us spent the remainder of the day taking it apart and trying to analyze the fault. The problem was that neither of us had much outboard motor repair experience. We eventually had to call HQ down in Saigon. A few days later, an 'expert' mechanic showed up, worked on the motor all afternoon, and pronounced it cured.

Beckman and Hebert analyzing engine

The following day several of us pushed the boat back off the beach and into the water. The two MP's who normally operated it jumped in, cranked it up, and took off for a test run. They hadn't gotten past the end of the dock when the engine blew up. Parts rained down for several minutes into the water.

The expert who had repaired it was on the phone arranging a ride to the airport at Tuy Hoa.

"Aren't you going to stay and help fix this?" asked Beckman. "Maybe we could send a diver down and retrieve a lot of the parts. It's not that deep there."

"Sorry, pal," he replied. "This is now beyond my expertise. You need a reality check and a new outboard!"

9. Recreation and Stupid Ideas

Recreation was essential to the men at Vung Ro. It helped alleviate the stress and boredom of being in a war zone. While there were no basketball, football, or baseball facilities, the soldiers at Vung Ro were lucky to engage in a sport not available to most other servicemen stationed in Vietnam: water skiing.

Water skiing behind a PBR

Kelly, the California surfer, somehow arranged to have a set of water skis fabricated in Qui Nhon by one of the 458th maintenance personnel responsible for fiberglass repair of the PBRs and Boston Whalers. Kelly forged the basic ski design from salvaged plywood, soaked it in water for a couple of days, and then bent the end of the wood to shape a set of skis. He drew an outline on the wood of the design he wanted. The crew in Qui Nhon then cut out the design, sanded, and fiber-glassed them.

SP-5 Beckman, the Sea Tigers Maintenance NCO, made frequent trips to Qui Nhon and managed to pick up the set of skis shortly after they had been fabricated. While not perfect from a professional standpoint, they were very well made and served their purpose quite well.

The crews took turns frolicking around the bay on the only known set of water skis on the Central Coast of Vietnam.

Another recreational highlight for the men of the 458th was auto racing, although not in the traditional vein.

One day an LST pulled in to Vung Ro Bay. They were a frequent sight in the bay, bringing supplies for the Air Force Base at Tuy Hoa. Typically, the deliveries were standard provisions and materials, but on one occasion, the LST was filled with various types of motorized equipment.

They spent the entire afternoon unloading and placing items in a secure, fenced-in area next to the PBR compound.

Charlie Rinslow was sitting on top of the PBR bunker watching the stevedores offload a few ¾-ton trucks, jeeps, a small tanker truck, a couple of backhoes, and three yellow airport tractor tugs, the little vehicles that are used to pull baggage carts around.

The tractor tugs intrigued Rinslow. He climbed down from the bunkers and made his way over across the sand to the holding area, where he approached a young stevedore who was busy securing some equipment.

"What are those for?" he inquired, pointing to the tractors.

"Don't know. We were just told to drop them off at Vung Ro. My guess is that they're for the air base—most of this stuff is going there. I think the Air Force is sending trucks down here tomorrow to pick it all up."

Later that evening, the LST finished offloading, pulled in the bow ramp, closed the bow doors, and backed off the beach. They turned to port and slowly steamed their way out of the harbor, everything on shore safely stored.

That night the tractors became the chattel of the 458th PBR boys when Rinslow and several others made their way over to the storage yard shortly after dark and found that none of the three tractors used keys. Rinslow hopped up onto the seat of one of them, pushed the 'start' button, and the engine sputtered to life. Releasing the brake, he pushed down on the gas pedal and took off, careening around the dirt yard. Encouraged by Rinslow, two other MPs fired up the remaining tractors and were soon racing them in circles and drag racing back and forth up and down the storage yard area. They ended up playing demolition derby with them well into the night, running them into one another time after time. They ran them so much that it was necessary to refuel them at one point, requiring Riggs and one of the other MPs to go back to the compound and fill up a couple of 5-gallon gas cans. The majority of the crew wound up over at the storage yard, not wanting to miss out on any of the adventures.

I was standing by the fence, watching the shenanigans, when the NCOIC showed up next to me.

"I heard a lot of commotion on my way to the head. What's going on here?"

"Just a little drag racing, Sarge," I answered.

He stood there, focused his sleepy eyes a bit, then shook his head. "I don't believe this. Sometimes I feel nothing more than a babysitter. I'm going back to bed."

He must have realized that it was much too late for him to intervene at that point, anyway.

By 3:00 or 4:00 am, two of the little tractors had blown their engines. The crew had revved the engines well beyond their acceptable limits during their night of reverie and mayhem. There was not much fun driving just one of them around, so we called it a night. Rinslow emerged as the demolition derby's victor and was cheered by all as we returned to our hootch.

The next day the Air Force showed up with several tractor-trailers to pick up all the equipment. Rinslow was standing nearby, watching everything being loaded. One of the drivers wanted to know what had happened to the tractor tugs. All were damaged, and two wouldn't even turn over and start.

"Don't rightly know," replied Rinslow. "Looks like the work of the VC to me!"

The Air Force left Vung Ro Bay with the totaled tractors. No one ever heard anything about them again.

The Racetrack

Every military unit in Vietnam seemed to have a dog or two. The companionship of a pet somehow eased the pain and harshness of having to spend a year in a war zone. Our dog was named Lady. She was there before I got there. She was there before Riggs got there. She was there before anybody got there. We guessed her to be six or seven years old at the most. One time she had a litter of puppies, five or six, I think. The entire unit became enthralled by the new additions to our family. We ensured they were very well taken care of, even letting them sleep inside the building, which was something Lady would never even dream of doing.

Some of the PBR puppies

One day Riggs noticed that the puppies always wanted to venture out on the beach and scamper about in the shallow water. Somehow, he came up with the brilliant idea of holding Puppy Races. We would each take a puppy and wade out to the end of the PBR pier, let it go, and see which one got to shore first. The distance was not extreme, and the dogs appeared to love it. The races soon became a gambling venue, with soldiers from all over the camp placing bets on their favorite canine.

As I recall, they were held every week for several weeks. Bit by bit, though, everyone began to tire of the same old thing.

Sitting in the dayroom, nursing his Olympia beer one afternoon, Riggs hatched another idea.

"Hey, suppose we taught the puppies how to parachute?"

"You've had too much to drink," McCall answered, laughing at the idea.

"No, No. I've been thinking. The mortar flares have pretty big 'chutes on them, much larger than the regular flares. I think they might hold a puppy."

Well, that was it. A couple of the guys went over to visit a perimeter guard who always enjoyed our hijinks. Soon after, they returned with a couple of small parachutes, and Airborne Puppy Training began.

Several of us decided that the safest place to launch the puppies would be from the top of the fuel tank platform.

"What if they get hurt landing?' I asked Riggs.

"I've already thought of that. We'll have a couple of guys with an Army blanket ready to catch them."

All went as planned except that the puppies weren't very fond of the training. As they floated gracefully to earth, they all had a look of sheer terror on their faces, so we terminated practice after only three puppies took flight.

Riggs finally gave up trying to teach the dogs anything other than everyday pet routines.

Puppy Parachute Training

■

We also had a monkey who lived with us for a long time. He was there before I arrived and, like Lady, the dog, no one could remember when or how he became one of us. He was a bit of a nuisance most of the time, though. During the daytime, he was relatively friendly, allowing us to pet him and even carry him around. At night, however, he would always retreat to the roof of our building. Whenever someone had to go to the bathroom during the night, he would jump down from the roof and land on your back, scaring us half to death. After many of these episodes, we would cautiously exit the hootch and run as we reached the door. We could usually hear him landing behind us.

One night, one of the MP's was on duty at the desk and had to go to the outhouse. As he was walking out, the monkey jumped on his back. He calmly reached up behind him, grabbed the animal, and threw it to the ground. Then he pulled his .45 caliber pistol and shot him.

Jinks the Monkey

The incident saddened many of us who had grown accustomed to the challenge of being attacked on our way to the outhouse. The NCOIC reprimanded the MP, but nothing else.

Young soldiers are, by the very nature of their youth, relatively stupid and naïve. This was the case when the U.S. Army placed four 18 and 19-years-olds on a high-speed boat outfitted with three .50-caliber machine guns, a Honeywell automatic grenade launcher that fires 250 grenades a minute, an M-79 grenade launcher, four M-16 assault rifles, a 12-gauge shotgun, four .45-caliber pistols, cases of concussion grenades, and a bottomless supply of ammunition. What a recipe for a sure-fire disaster! Skipping across the water at speeds in excess of 30 knots, it was only a matter of time before they found trouble—or trouble found them.

PBR on patrol

In short, the youthful crew of the 458th enjoyed making things explode. One of our favorite activities was blowing up wooden grenade boxes. It required a team of three: one to operate the PBR and get it up to full speed, another to hold an empty wooden grenade box over the stern, and then a third to drop a concussion grenade into the box and shut the lid. Then it would be thrown off the back of the speeding boat, float in the wake for a moment, and then blow up, sending hundreds of splinters flying everywhere and creating a thunderous *Boom!*

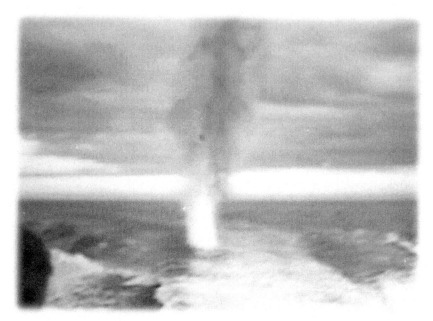

Wooden grenade box explosion

I was standing in the radio room talking to the MP on duty when the radio blared out.

"Base, base, this is PBR 29." It was McCall, calling on the PRC-25 radio mounted in his boat.

"29, this is base, over," answered the MP.

"Base, tell Beckman we're coming in. We need to put *Captain America* on the beach immediately. I think we hit a rock across the bay. There's a large hole in the stern, and we're taking on water. We're sinking!"

"Roger that, 29. I'll go get him," the MP said.

"Three-two, can you watch the radio for me for a second?"

Beckman arrived a short time later.

"Somethings weird, here, Three-two," he said after granting permission for the beaching. "McCall knows this bay and surrounding waters better than anyone, and I know the bay almost as well, and I can't think of any rocks they could have hit."

"Yeah, I don't have any idea, either," I said.

McCall nosed the boat onto the soft sand, and a couple of the off-duty crew came out and secured lines to the waiting bulldozer that Beckman had requisitioned from one of the other units. When everything was connected, the bulldozer dragged the PBR up onto the beach.

A few days later, HQ sent a fiberglass professional down from Qui Nhon to fix the damage. He was there for over a week repairing the hull.

Beckman, ever curious, kept badgering McCall until he finally confessed the truth.

"Well, I guess we were the victims of a grenade box explosion gone wrong," he confessed. "All was going according to plan: One of the MPs opened the grenade box and held it over the stern, then the other MP pulled the pin on a grenade and dropped it into the box."

Unfortunately, the MP holding the box neglected to throw it far enough astern. The motion of a water-jet propelled PBR moving through the water tends to create a vortex directly behind the stern, which extends a couple of feet beyond the back of the boat. The box had been sucked back into the rear of the boat, and that's where it had exploded.

On another occasion, an MP from Louisiana thought he could do a bit better than just blowing up a wooden crate. He was very curious to see just how big a splash he could make. One afternoon while out on patrol, the coxswain decided to put the boat in neutral and just drift around, as they did on most patrols. The MP went to the engine hatch area, opened a case of grenades, and removed a handful. He tied ten concussion grenades together, using one in the center as a detonator. He carried the device up to the bow—setting it off as he went—intending to throw it overboard at the last minute.

The wake generated by a PBR

Making his way to the bow, he tripped on the starboard cleat and fell to the deck, next to the .50-caliber gun tub. The grenades fell from his hands, landing just under the lip of the gun tub.

Scrambling to his feet, the MP managed to retrieve the grenades and quickly threw them overboard. They exploded about 5 feet from the boat and under about a foot of water.

PBR "Captain America" on the beach

The explosive force of the combined 10 pounds of TNT was tremendous, lifting the bow of the 16,000-pound vessel at least two feet in the air. The crew thought for sure that the bow had been blown away, but to the manufacturer's credit, the boat was intact.

They never tried anything like that again.

One night we were out on patrol, and a firefight ensued on shore. We positioned ourselves at one end of the bay and commenced saturating the area with machine gun fire. Flares were shot off by the bunker guards, hoping to spot the enemy. I heard a loud *thud* at one point during the event.

"What was that?" I asked Kelly.

"Beats me. I heard it, too, though. Everything looks OK."

Illumination flare in the deck of PBR 32

At the end of our shift, we returned to the dock and secured the boat. It wasn't until the next day that we noticed an illumination flare that had been fired from one of the bunkers the night before. It had gone through the bow deck, which in and of itself didn't mean much as the structure of the vessel wasn't compromised. It was just strange to have it embedded into our boat.

10. The Merchant Marine

Merchant Marine cargo ships visited the bay frequently. Bombs, napalm, bullets, weapons, fuel, and just about all the other tools of war had to be delivered by ship. Vessels would stay in port for an average of two days while stevedores from Vung Ro off-loaded their cargo onto tractor-trailer trucks for transport over the mountains to the US Air Base at Tuy Hoa or the Army camp at Phu Hiep. Oil tankers would moor off to a floating 4-point anchor system consisting of large buoys and a pipeline pump-out. The Viet Cong would, on occasion, attempt to send in swimmers, known as "sappers," to place underwater explosives on the hulls of the ships, hoping to blow them up. The 458th PBRs were tasked with providing security for the visiting ships by escorting them in and out of the harbor and providing dockside security while they were at the pier. This consisted of regular patrols around the DeLong Pier. Concussion grenades would be dropped overboard at staggered intervals to deter or kill enemy swimmers attempting to attack the ships.

"Always be on the lookout for suspicious sampans lurking around outside the bay whenever ships are in port," McCall told me. "The Viet Cong use them as spotters. Then they can plan to move stuff around since they know we'll be busy guarding the ships. They will run weapons-laden sampans right across the mouth of the bay and know that we can't go after them."

He also told me that the Viet Cong would sometimes blow a hole in the pipeline leading over the mountains to the Air Force base. They knew that any interruption in the delivery of fuel would disrupt the activities of the jet fighters, helicopters, and other aircraft stationed there.

It was customary for the visiting ships to invite the PBR crews aboard for lunch or dinner. The majority of vessels were American-flagged and crewed by Americans. They always treated us very well and fed us like kings. Steaks were in plentiful supply on the ships, something we rarely had in our mess hall. In turn, for being well-fed, we would reciprocate by dropping the required loads of concussion grenades further away from their steel ships, thereby reducing the bone-rattling jar that accompanied such activity. The ships' crews dreaded the nightly concussion grenade runs. It was virtually impossible to get a decent night's sleep, so the farther out the grenade drop, the better.

Cargo Ship "TransCaribbean" delivering a load of bombs

Some ships, however, were chartered from other countries, usually the Philippines. They were crewed by Filipinos who neglected to feed the PBR crews. For some reason, they seemed to need increased security at night, usually at around 3:00 am. The PBR crews would run right up alongside the hull and drop grenades all along the length of the ship. The noise inside the steel hull of the cargo ships was deafening. Getting any sleep at all was out of the question.

One afternoon we spent a considerable amount of time during our shift engaged in our favorite pastime—fishing. We came back to the dock late in the afternoon with a large number of fish and clams.

Riggs met us at the pier and eyed our catch. "You know, it's about time for another barbeque on the beach. Why don't one of you go over to the fuel tanker at the pier and see what you can trade some of this stuff for?"

"Good idea," I said. "I'll run right over there."

We packed up a few large fish and a lot of clams. One of the other guys helped me carry everything, and we made our way over to the ship and found the cook.

After brief introductions, I made our pitch. "I've got three boxes of fresh-caught fish of all different varieties, plus a large bag of Vung Ro clams. What do you think you might want to trade for?"

The MP who went with me helped me carry the 20 prime steaks and a 5-gallon tub of chocolate ice cream back to the compound.

When we got back, the grill was ready, and the beers were flowing. It turned out that Riggs was also a pretty decent barbeque guy. The evening was spent with a couple of us playing guitars and singing songs around the fire Riggs had built on the beach. The ice cream was incredible.

It made me think of my old Boy Scout days as a kid.

Fuel tanker "Saumico" at anchor in Vung Ro Bay

Tugboat assisting cargo ship alongside Delong pier

Cargo ship unloading at Delong Pier

11. The MIUWS Attack

I walked into the dayroom. It was hot outside, unbearably hot. The water of the bay was mirror-like, still, and placid. There was not a breath of wind anywhere.

I needed a beer.

Riggs was at it again, over in a corner surrounded by a small group of eager listeners.

"Back in '68, on my first tour here," he was saying, "we ran LARC's into this place. We would offload ships and bring the cargo to shore, where it would be offloaded and sent by truck up the coast. The Navy had a small team of undersea warfare guys stationed up the hill—must have been about 30 of them, as I remember. They had a couple of gunboats and a Boston Whaler here. They were in charge of the water-side security for the base back then."

I smiled. Riggs loved telling a story, and this sounded like the beginning of a good one.

"I got to know this one guy real well; Chip Schaefer was his name. We used to hang out together all the time—both being from Minnesota. One day he and another MIUWS guy showed up at our hootch with a damn cooked lizard! Seems like Schaefer and his buddy—J.P, I think his name was—had been down at the far end of the beach, and they ran into a small group of South Koreans who were barbecuing a 6-foot monitor lizard just outside the concertina wire. They were invited over and spent the afternoon drinking beer and eating. On their way back to their hootch, they dropped off some leftovers to me. Best damn lizard I ever ate!"

"Wait a minute. What's MIUS," one of the group asked.

"It's MIUWS, and it stands for Mobile Inshore Undersea Warfare Surveillance. They left here just after I arrived."

He continued with, "Anyway, I had a hard time sleeping that night. I remember it well. It must have been about 12:30 am. It was a cool night, unusual for Vietnam. The sky was overcast, which shut out the moonlight. I remember it being a very dark night."

The story was getting interesting. I grabbed my cold beer and went and sat down with the group, waiting to hear what might happen next.

"My friend, Schaefer, and three of his buddies, including J.P, were on duty in the communications bunker that night. Schaefer said they were all standing around, drinking hot coffee."

A couple of the younger GI's squirmed nervously in their seats. All eyes were glued to Riggs. He could tell a good story.

"Anyway, it was dark as hell out. Schaefer said that he had been looking out of the bunker, out across the bay, when he glimpsed a bright flash out of the corner of his eye. His buddy, J.P, raised his arms instinctively to protect himself. The explosion blasted Schaefer to the floor. An RPG had hit their bunker. He found his M-16, sat up, chambered a round, and fired into the night. Although darkness hid the sapper, there was sufficient backlight from the beach, and his bullet dropped the guy. Then another RPG came in."

The troops were fidgeting in nervous anticipation. A couple more guys had come in and sat down, bringing the group to over a half-dozen. This was one of Riggs' better stories.

"Schaefer said he was immobilized. He heard voices... loud voices. One was his friend, Tom, who was hurt real bad from the explosion. He was screaming for J.P. to help him. The other voice was J.P. screaming at Tom to be quiet. They all knew the drill. After the frag, Charlie would enter the bunker to finish off anyone left alive. Well, sure enough, the gooks came in shooting, and as their bullets tore into Tom, his screaming stopped. Two or three slugs went into this other guy, Max, who was already dead. J.P. was next. Each time the guns fired, Schaefer said he could see silhouettes. A muzzle moved and pointed at him."

"He told me that he realized that it was his time to meet death. He said he had two vivid memories: his life would be over at 21, and the other that his mother would be heartbroken. He said he felt calm and peace, and then the moment passed."

There was total silence in the room. I thought a couple of the guys had tears in their eyes, but it was hard to tell.

"Anyway, Schaefer realized that he was still alive! He couldn't understand it. In Charlie's haste to grab all of their weapons, Schaefer had been spared. He lay there in the dark, quietly having beaten death. One of his knuckles had been shot off, and he had been hit with shrapnel. He didn't know what to do next. Time became his new enemy. He didn't know how bad his injuries were, and he was passing in and out of consciousness. He told me he felt like he was drifting through a twilight zone."

"Finally, he heard the reassuring sound of American voices as several armed soldiers burst into the bunker."

"In addition to their bunker, several guard towers had been attacked. The dead and wounded were trucked to the beach where a chopper had already landed to transport the wounded. The door gunner strapped Schaefer into a seat behind an M-60 machine gun. The casualties were stacked together, and they lifted off. Although the sky was filled with the sound of machine guns and tracers, Schaefer said that everything seemed quiet to him. The door gunner was busy on the floor, doing whatever he could for the wounded as the chopper banked out of harm's way."

"When the chopper got to Tuy Hoa Medevac Hospital, the door gunner jumped to the ground before the landing struts even touched down. Medics, doctors, and grunts were everywhere. Someone signaled for Schaefer to carry one end of a stretcher. He said they carried it inside and placed it on a table. A medic took Schaefer's arm and asked where the holes were, but he said he couldn't understand him. The medic led him to a sink, handed him a bar of soap, and mimed for him to clean himself up. He said he would find the holes."

"Schaefer said that doctors and nurses were all bent over tables holding the wounded men as they tried to save them. He saw two medics carry his friend Tom past the tables. He was stacked in the corner with the dead."

"Later, he woke up in the intensive care unit to the sound of a wavering moan. His ears were ringing as he turned and saw a young man in the next gurney. Schaefer said his face was unmarked, with no wounds, no acne scars, no blemishes at all. He looked like a boy, Schaefer told me, maybe a high school quarterback. His mouth was moving, though. He was screaming. Below the perfect face was a full-body cast exposing only fingers and toes. Schaefer said he tried to call for help, but medics had already rushed to his side. A nurse explained that the boy's cast was too tight. Schaefer watched as they cut through the plaster, and his screaming stopped."

"Sit tight. I'll be right back," Riggs said as he jumped up out of his chair and made a beeline for the refrigerator.

"OK, so they rolled Schaefer into a ward, and he was reunited with J.P. in the ICU the next day. Schaefer didn't know J.P. had survived, but both his hands had been blown off. Schaefer said he put his hand on J.P's remaining arm, and they both cried, the tears coming from their souls. They tried to talk, but both had lost their eardrums. A unit of whole blood led to J.P's jugular. He would be going home soon."

"Schaefer asked the nurse if the boy in the body cast would be going home, but she told him that his wounds were too severe for him to be moved."

"Later that day, Schaefer remembered, this doctor—a full bird colonel—stood in the middle of the ward and called out names. A medic handed a box to each patient on the list, and the colonel saluted him. The GI's were told that, on behalf of the United States of America, they were awarded the Purple Heart for wounds received in combat."

Riggs hesitated for just a moment. "You guys won't believe this next part." Some moved their chairs a little closer.

"Schaefer said that as this colonel passed his bed, he gave him a sympathetic look. He didn't get a Purple Heart! The colonel knew he should have one, but Schaefer was Navy, not Army. His would have to come through Navy channels."

"You're kidding." One of the young soldiers seated next to me said.

"Anyway, Schaefer said that night, after supper, the doctor returned and presented him with a Purple Heart. It had been the medal intended for the boy in the body cast. He had died. Schaefer told me that he was thinking of the night he had been wounded. He thought of his dead friends and the boy in the body cast. He thought about their families receiving letters of condolence."

"When it was Schaefer's time to go home, the colonel shook his hand and handed him an envelope containing his medical records and orders. The medic also shook his hand

and wished him well. He gave him a Red Cross box containing a Bible, toiletries, and cigarettes."

"Schaefer left Vietnam wearing pajamas, a faded blue bathrobe, and shower shoes. His only possessions were the envelope, the Red Cross box... and the young soldier's Purple Heart."

12. Sergeant ROK

No one knew his real name. The name tag on his shirt was in Korean. He was called Sergeant ROK, from the acronym for the Republic of Korea. He was a crew chief on a South Korean gun truck stationed high up on the bluff above Vung Ro Bay. Sergeant ROK was very proud of his truck, one of the few in the entire area outfitted with quadruple .50-caliber electric-fire machine guns. He made frequent trips down to the bay to show it off. He sat in a central pod above the guns, which enabled him to control all of them simultaneously. It was a weapon of immense firepower.

Sergeant ROK

Rumor around the base was that Sergeant ROK was a man of substantial wealth back home in Seoul, having made a small fortune in brass, most of it coming from Vung Ro Bay, Signal Mountain, and the Korean Compound.

South Korean Guntruck with quad .50's

Sergeant ROK was a friendly, outgoing young entrepreneur who appeared to have many Korean soldiers working for him. Whenever one of the PBRs returned from a fire mission, it seemed like one of Sergeant ROK's men would show up soon after that, bartering with Riggs for the expended brass casings that were always covering the decks of the patrol boats. The more enterprising MPs of the unit were known to fire many more rounds than necessary during a mission, simply to have more to barter with upon their return to the dock.

If you wanted anything decent in Vietnam, you had to trade for it—plain and simple. Once a week or so, Sergeant

ROK would show up to visit Fat Cook with sandbags full of rock lobster and depart with boxes of hamburger patties.

■

Two Korean soldiers were aboard the *Magic Christian,* shoveling brass casings into empty sandbags. McCall and I were sitting on the bow with Riggs, discussing the barter offered to us: a .45-caliber grease gun, which was a light, compact machine gun.

"It sounds like a good deal to me," I said. "We can come up with another twelve bags of shells easily. We'll just go out tonight and attack some rocks or something."

The deal was for twenty sandbags of brass casings. The Koreans had shoveled almost eight bags already.

"We can have that much in the next couple of days," McCall said.

"I don't know," I countered. "I wonder if the honchos down at headquarters ever wonder why we requisition so much ammunition. They must think Vung Ro Bay is a real hot spot!"

We all laughed. The two Koreans had finished loading the sandbagged brass and came up to Riggs.

"So, G.I., we have deal?"

Riggs got up, walked to the gunwale, and stepped off the boat onto the small dock. "Sure, we can do that. We'll have the rest of the brass by the end of the week—Friday, OK?"

"Yes, good. We bring gun then." They shook hands, and the two soldiers each grabbed up two sandbags and started shuttling the brass to their deuce-and-a-half, parked out front.

■

Later that month, the Viet Cong blew the fuel pipeline near Hwy QL-1, just above the turn-off leading to Vung Ro. Fuel gushed out and soon covered our road. A truck loaded with Koreans was coming down to the bay to go swimming when the driver hit the slick roadway, careened over the embankment, and crashed.

An hour or so later, Sgt. ROK showed up at our compound with a deuce-and-a-half truck loaded with the victims on several stretchers. Some were covered completely.

"Several dead," he told our NCOIC. "Many more injured. We have medevacs coming soon."

Two more trucks arrived with more wounded. Sgt. ROC had all the dead and wounded waiting by the helipad.

Not thirty minutes later, two medevac helicopters touched down, loaded up all the stretchers, and flew off.

"This is very sad day," said Sgt. ROC as he downed a beer in our dayroom. "I must write letters to many mothers today."

13. The Great Beer Heist

It didn't take me long to learn that this was no ordinary Army unit. Very early one morning, there came a frantic knock at my door. "Wake up, Three-two. Wake up!"

Rising from a much-needed sleep, I swung my legs out over the edge of my bunk, sweat already running down my back. I silently cursed the hot metal Quonset hut, got up and walked over to the door, noticing my alarm clock read 3:00 AM. It was Charlie Rinslow, the MP from Oakland, California.

"You've got to come with me! We need all the help we can get."

He seemed very desperate, so I got dressed as fast as possible, smiled at the Mystery Girl inside my locker, and followed him out of the Quonset hut. "What's going on, Chuck? Why are you waking me up so early?"

"You'll see."

We walked in the dark of night across the 100 or so yards separating the PBR compound from the fenced-in cargo holding area at the top of the concrete boat ramp.

There were quite a few large Conex's, wooden pallets with everything imaginable stacked on them, and even two brand-new jeeps.

Rinslow was babbling on and on about a ship and darkness and beer.

The two of us made our way inside the secure holding area and walked around the back of some pallets piled high with supplies. Several of the MPs from the PBR detachment were already there, removing the cardboard from two pallets.

I was perplexed.

"What's going on?" I asked, looking around, trying to assess the situation.

More men from the PBR barracks were coming in right behind us. Before long, just about every man in the unit was there, standing around wondering what this was all about.

LST (Landing Ship Tank) offloading supplies at night

"We had an LST come in last night," Riggs explained. "They were supposed to be here earlier in the day but had engine problems. Anyway, they got it fixed, but that made them arrive here after dark, making them very uncomfortable. They had to offload their cargo and get out of here. They were worried about getting attacked, just sitting on the beach all night. The trucks can't move the cargo to Tuy Hoa until daylight, so the ship's captain asked us to guard the supplies overnight since we're the only MPs around."

Then he started getting excited. "They off-loaded several tractor-trailer loads of supplies. We posted two guards, and then the ship untied her lines, backed off the beach, and left. After a couple of hours, one of the guys got nosy and started snooping around at all the pallets of stuff and found twelve pallets of beer—Pabst Blue Ribbon and Olympia. All going to Tuy Hoa Air Force Base!"

By the time the sun had come up, only ten pallets of beer had remained in the secure holding area. The rest, 144 cases in all, had been carried to the PBR compound, two cases at a time. It was stashed under bunks, inside lockers, inside the bunker, on top of the shower, onboard the PBRs, and even buried in the soft beach sand.

I figured that we had stolen 3,456 cans of beer! We had "appropriated" two entire pallets, one Pabst Blue Ribbon and one of Olympia.

I was sure we would all be going to jail for several years. "Don't worry about it, man," Riggs told me after I expressed my concern. "We *are* the cops!"

The following morning all the supplies were loaded aboard trucks and taken north to the Air Force Base. To make themselves feel better, all agreed that had the beer been destined for the Army guys at Phu Hiep, they more than likely wouldn't have taken it. But the Air Force was a different story. I knew better. I chuckled at this self-serving rationalization as I realized that I was working with a bunch of crooks, and they had now made me an accomplice.

Of course, I wasn't complaining all that much. After all, it was free beer!

After a hasty meeting the next morning, we agreed to confess our sins to the NCOIC. He took it better than we expected. As a matter of fact, he even smiled.

A couple of days later, two investigators from the Air Force Office of Special Investigations (OSI) showed up. Our NCOIC, an Army MP with a penchant for the stolen beverage, handled the inquiry, and a short time later, the investigators departed. I never knew what transpired in their conversation, but nothing more was ever said about it.

The crew of the 458th devised a plan to sell beer to themselves, at 10 cents a can, and other Vung Ro soldiers. The lowly dayroom soon became a full-fledged bar. At the end of each month, we would all split the profits. We made enough money to purchase stereos, dorm-sized refrigerators for our rooms, and pretty much whatever else we wanted.

I remodeled my room with paneling made from the two empty pallets. I staggered the boards, stained them, bought a refrigerator, a Sony cassette deck, a reel-to-reel tape deck, a Minolta camera, and sent my mother some expensive oriental lamps.

Business was good. Very, very good.

■

There were only two seasons in the Central Highlands: rainy and wet or dry and hot. The dry season was February to April.

At most times of the year, the heat in Vietnam was unbearable. The air was so humid that we wore as little as possible, most days nothing but cut-off shorts and sometimes a t-shirt. Some of the guys went bare-chested, but I hated the sweat dripping down my chest. I found that even a t-shirt soaked in sweat tended to provide some absorbency.

On top of the humidity was the heat; it was unrelentingly hot in Vung Ro Bay. Even the birds found shelter somewhere. Flies found a cool spot to take a nap, and fish discovered nice big rocks under which to hide.

We would sweat, sweat, and sweat some more. Daily salt pills became a necessity of life.

.

The monsoon season arrived with a vengeance in early June. It arrived with an intensity that I had never anticipated nor experienced. It rained, and rained, and rained: incessantly and relentlessly, day after day after day, usually for several hours, sometimes longer. It rained as hard as one could ever imagine for over six months. It was as if someone had turned the ocean upside down and dumped it on us.

I was captivated by the monsoons. I couldn't believe it could rain so hard for so long. During the year I was there, we had 94" of rain. I had given up wearing any semblance of a uniform a long time ago, and the rains only proved that a uniform was a bad idea. I wore cutoff shorts, a T-shirt, and sometimes deck shoes. If it were raining a lot, I would go barefoot. It was muddy and slippery everywhere, anyway.

The sun rarely came out. Each day we woke up to a lifeless and gloomy day, gray and dreary, and it stayed that way until darkness enveloped us at night. It was just one miserable day after another.

On one occasion, we were preparing to go out on patrol. The other PBR was coming in ahead of a ferocious band of rain moving in from the ocean. I watched as the storm moved towards us from across the bay. I heard thunder rumbling to the East, slowly at first, then increasing in intensity. Forked lightning crackled in the distance and lit up the sky.

McCall's boat and crew arrived dockside just as my crew and I fired up the engines and made our way out into the bay, all the while keeping a sharp eye out on the approaching weather. As we got further out into the water, I realized that the rain had a distinct wall around it. I increased speed and ventured into the ocean to meet the incoming band of rain and drove my PBR around it without ever getting wet.

That's the way it was with monsoon rain. It came down in literal sheets, sometimes in narrow bands, sometimes in broad areas.

We learned that the best thing to do during monsoon season was to hide out somewhere. Going out on patrol in the PBRs meant fighting biting wind and rain for an entire shift. The best thing to do was tie up to a buoy and wait for your shift to be over.

We also learned that the Viet Cong liked to plan most of their activities and troop movements during the monsoon season. The Americans didn't like the misery of the never-ending torrential rains. Neither had the French.

The Viet Cong grew up in it.

Then suddenly, one afternoon, the clouds drifted away, and the sun came out, acting as if nothing had ever happened.

14. Exploring

There's something about a cave that attracts boys and men of all ages. The island of Hon Nua, a mere 5 kilometers southeast of Vung Ro Bay, was the source of such an attraction. It was a small island, a lone sentinel dotting the sea, prohibiting passage from the south, uninhabited, with a sharply sloping hill on one side and a rocky promontory dominating the other.

Island of Hon Nua, viewed from Hwy QL-1

While technically outside our patrol area, we decided to invent some story to justify visiting the island soon after Beckman arrived in Vung Ro.

What mysteries did this little island hold? We were excited about what we might find: evidence of Viet Cong occupation, bones of previous visitors, or even buried treasure.

The PBRs were much too large for any outings to the island, so the small Boston Whaler's with 40-hp Johnson outboards had to be utilized.

Early one Saturday morning Johnny Dees, Beckman, Kelly, and I walked out on the lopsided PBR dock and loaded up the little Boston Whaler with some C-rations, water, M-16's and an M-79 grenade launcher. We were dressed only in cutoff shorts, flip-flops, and Boonie hats. None of us wore a shirt. The morning mist was struggling to let the daylight invade.

The 40-hp Johnson outboard didn't want to start, as was the norm. I primed it and pulled the cord again, this time with a bit more force. After a few more tries, it sputtered, coughed, gasped for fuel, belched a cloud of blue smoke, and sprang to life.

Dees and Beckman untied the lines as I put the little craft into gear, the engine protesting with a noticeable "clunk" as the transmission engaged. Dees and Beckman sat in the bow, and we headed south towards the DeLong Pier.

The boat sat low in the water with the four passengers. Typically, we only operated them with two people, allowing them to perform at a relatively decent speed.

"This is going to take a while," I commented. "We're only doing about 10 knots. Some of you guys need to go on a diet!"

We had passed the pier and were making our way towards the ship mooring buoys when one of the PBRs came barreling towards us, returning from a night patrol. McCall was at the helm and slowed his boat briefly as he passed.

"Where are you idiots going?" was all I could hear above the roar of the big diesels as McCall opened up the throttles again. The wake sent us all bouncing around in the little boat. I hoped no water came over the bow—that would spell trouble with all the weight we had in the boat. Luckily, none did, and we proceeded on, passing the mouth of Vung Ro Bay and sailing into the coastal waters of the South China Sea.

The water was calm and quiet. It was going to be a beautiful day. It was my first visit to the cave. I was a bit apprehensive, not knowing what we might find there. I prayed that it wasn't being used as a secret Viet Cong base camp or something.

Cave on the island of Hon Nua

We arrived at the island of Hon Nua, slowed to idle speed, and motored around to the far side of the island. The south side was jagged rock with sheer cliffs caused by a constant battering of easterly swells from the South China Sea. The leeward side, however, was calm and offered a small cave accessible only at low tide.

"Looks like we timed this one just right," said Beckman. "The tide's just about perfect for us to get into the cave. We've probably got a good window of some three or four hours."

"Yeah, but we'll need to clear it out first," added Johnny Dees. "Get me up closer, Three-two, and I'll drop a shot in there."

I guided the small boat up with care to the cave entrance, about 20 feet from the opening. "Close enough?" I yelled as I put the outboard engine into neutral.

Dees had loaded an M-79 grenade into the hand-held launcher. He steadied himself with one leg on the bow of the boat, aimed the launcher, and fired one round into the small, dark cave. The explosion was deafening and echoed throughout the small cave. None of us had expected the noise to be so intense.

"You might want to back up a bit!" hollered Dees, just as hundreds of black bats came swarming out of the mouth of the cave, upset and angry that their peaceful grotto had been invaded.

We watched in amazement as bats flew off in a frenzy towards the other side of the island.

"OK, it should be all clear, now. Let's go on in." Beckman suggested. "I think that's probably got them all spooked for a few hours."

I put the boat in gear and slowly motored into the cave. The sides of the Whaler scraped the walls in several places. "Keep your hands in the boat!" I yelled.

We tied the boat off to a small boulder jutting out from the side of the cave. Leaving our weapons in the boat, we all stepped out into the small cave's shallow waters to explore the surrounding area. It was dark inside. Just a sliver of sunlight shone into the cave from an overhead shaft. I was glad Dees had scattered all the bats. It was tranquil, almost scary, in a sense. I looked around as best I could. It was cool in the cave. Cool and quiet. It offered an unspoken sanctuary. A place to hide from the war, a place to hide until it was time to go home.

"I'm going up on top," I declared after having investigated all there was to see inside the cave. Wading out of the cave in waist-deep water, I made my way to a tiny strip of sand just outside the entrance.

"Wait for us—we're all going!" Dees yelled, his words echoing in the hollow of the cave. We all waded out, the boat secure and hidden in its rock-lined garage.

One by one, we started the climb up the steep rocky face of the island. It was a slow trek. The rock was jagged and slippery in spots, but we took our time and were very careful. None of us wanted to get medevac'd if we fell. That would have been very hard to explain.

We all stood together at the summit, feeling as if we'd just conquered Mt. McKinley. The hot sun was getting high in the sky. Our adventure had taken the better part of the morning. We were all standing there, taking in the sheer beauty of the small rocky island. It was a peaceful break from the war. I looked out into the ocean. The South China Sea went on forever.

Our trance was suddenly interrupted by the distant sounds of a Huey helicopter. The familiar *whop-whop-whop* was unmistakable. The four of us looked out from the top of the island, far to the south, and saw two Huey gunships heading our way, the minigun pods hanging menacingly off to either side of the fuselage. We stood there, in the blazing sun, watching the choppers getting closer and closer. It appeared that their course might take them right over the island itself.

"Oh damn!" muttered Beckman, breaking the revered silence we had all been enjoying. "We don't have any uniforms on!"

"What are you talking about?" asked Kelly.

"We don't have any uniforms on. The choppers—they'll think we're Viet Cong!"

Suddenly realizing that Beckman had a very valid point, we scattered quickly. It was too slow a process to attempt to get back down the cliff face, so we ran and hid under or behind whatever we could find. There were a few large boulders that afforded some shelter, and two of us hid there. However, we would have to move around the boulders as the choppers passed to avoid them seeing us.

"Is everyone OK?" asked Beckman. As an E-5, he was the senior man in the group and, if anything happened, he knew he would be the one facing the music.

One by one, we all acknowledged our safety. Hopefully well hidden, we awaited the passing of the helicopters. The rotor noise became louder and louder. The two helicopters flew low over the tiny island. I felt like I probably could have peered out from my hiding place and looked right into the face of the chopper pilot.

The choppers flew right over the top of us, continued for about a quarter-mile, and then one of them abruptly turned around.

"Damn," yelled Beckman. "Are all of you hidden well? They're coming back!"

None of us wanted to be the recipient of fire spitting from the helicopter's mini-guns. For a moment, I thought of suggesting everyone step into the open and raise their hands in surrender.

"What should we do?" screamed Johnny Dees from his spot behind one of the boulders.

"Nothing, just yet—wait and see what he does. But if he fires even one shot, jump out into the open and surrender."

"That won't work, Lee," shouted Kelly. "Mini-guns don't fire single shots! We'll be dead before we can raise our hands!"

The lone chopper was almost upon us.

"Just dig in, then. And pray!" Beckman tried to squirm his way deeper into the hard soil. He was hiding next to a small rock. "If that pilot looks hard enough, he's going to see me. I don't know, guys; maybe we should surrender."

The helicopter was just approaching the edge of the island and then, for no apparent reason, turned around again and flew back towards the other chopper.

All four of us breathed a heavy sigh of relief.

"What the hell was he up to?" Kelly asked Beckman.

"I have no idea—don't want to find out either. Let's get out of here while we're still alive!"

With extreme caution, we crawled down the face of the small cliff and scrambled to the boat. Dees untied the line. I fired up the cranky old Johnson and backed slowly out of the cave. We had planned on eating our lunch of C-rations on the island. All of a sudden, nobody was hungry.

No one spoke during the long journey back. Beckman appeared lost in thought: things could very easily have gone horribly wrong. Someone had been watching over us, no doubt.

Arriving back at the docks, we tied the boat up behind McGraw's PBR and proceeded straight to the dayroom.

We needed a drink.

15. Retiring Old Betsy

Riggs had the hood up on the old ¾-ton truck. He was sprawled out across the top of the engine, his hands deep in the bowels of the engine compartment, turning, twisting, screwing, unscrewing, pulling, and pushing.

He was in a foul mood. "Damn this piece of crap! I'm getting tired of having to fix this damn thing every time we want to go to Tuy Hoa."

A hammer appeared from nowhere. *Bang-Bang-Bang!*

I just stood there, watching the commotion, afraid to say too much of anything. It was very rare to see Riggs in a bad mood.

The old truck was well past its retirement date. It had been assigned to us because nobody else wanted it. And, they knew that we wouldn't bitch about it being so far removed from civilization.

Give it to the Vung Ro guys—they'll take anything.

I stared at the faded white star on the driver's door. It was barely recognizable anymore, yet still stood out in the noonday sun, a sad symbol of grander days on the road. It was time for the old truck to go.

Bang-Bang-Bang!

"Damn this piece of crap!"

After more than an hour of tinkering, Riggs got the old girl fired up. It coughed and sputtered, not happy with being brought to life.

Riggs jumped into the driver's seat and gave the old truck some gas. After the engine settled down to a rough idle, he hopped out again.

"OK, if you're going to town, get moving!" Riggs yelled out.

He was in the process of gathering up the tools. He was about to return them to the maintenance shed when he stopped, turned around, and placed them in the back of the truck.

"What's that for?" I asked.

"Never know. We might need them."

A half dozen of us boarded the old truck, and we set off for the hour ride over the mountains to Tuy Hoa.

Arriving at the base, Riggs dropped all of us off at the snack bar. "I'll meet you guys here soon." He drove off with no further explanation: the old truck spitting, coughing, and wheezing down the road.

Riggs showed up at the snack bar about an hour later, sporting a big grin across his lean and skinny face. "I've solved our transportation problem," he announced, proud of himself.

We all jumped up from the table and hurried outside. There, sporting the faded green bumpers of the 127th MP Company, stood a brand new ¾-ton truck—well, brand new to us!

"What the hell!" Beckman couldn't believe his eyes. "Did you get it painted?"

"Nope, just exchanged it for a better one."

Ever the con man, Riggs had ridden around the Air Force base until he spotted a ¾-ton truck that he liked. He parked next to it, went to the back of our truck, and got whatever tools he needed. Then he just switched bumpers—front and back. Since the bumper markings were the only unit identification of a vehicle, we knew it would be challenging for the Air Force to track down their missing truck.

Besides, we gave them Old Betsy—what more could they want?

The ride back to Vung Ro Bay was a joy. The new truck drove like a Cadillac. The OD green paint shined like it had a fresh wash and wax. There was a reassuring steady hum from the large knobby tires. Even the wood that fabricated the bench seats in the bed was fresh and new, not broken and rotted like in Old Betsy.

One of the new MPs, a fresh arrival from the States and on his first outing with us, couldn't quite figure it all out. "How did you get the keys?" he asked.

Laughter engulfed the back of the truck. The kid got a puzzled look on his face, realized he'd asked something stupid, and his face turned red.

"Military vehicles don't have keys," Riggs answered through the back window flap. "All they have is an off-on switch."

"We'll have to repaint the faded bumpers when we get back to the bay," I said to Riggs, changing the subject to save the kid some embarrassment.

"It's already on the list, man. Already on the list."

16. The Donut Dollies

I loved the rain, as long as I wasn't out in it. I liked listening to the raindrops splattering against the tin roof of the Quonset hut. *Ping-Ping-Ping!*

I was awakened just before dawn by a deafening crack of thunder. I got up out of my sweat-soaked bed and peered out my little window. Sweeping across the bay from the east was a severe thunderstorm, dark and sinister-looking. Raindrops started falling on the tin roof of the Quonset hut, soft little splats at first, and then the splats became heavier and louder as the intensity increased. It didn't take long until the sky let loose with all its fury—right on top of us. I was hoping the deluge might cool things off a bit, but I knew better. After the rain stopped, I knew that the ensuing humidity would be unbearable.

Welcome to Vietnam.

I decided that there was nothing I could do about the situation, so I lay back down on my bed and listened to the rain pounding on the roof, trying its best to get in through whatever cracks were available.

Breakfast turned out to be another disaster—what's new? Sometimes I felt like choking Fat Cook but then realized that it wasn't his fault. He was trying to do the best with what he had available. I wonder, though, if he even ate his own food.

I had just finished my last forkful of scrambled eggs when the door to the mess hall burst open, and one of the bunker guards rushed in. He was overflowing with excitement.

"I just found out from Qui Nhon that we're getting some Red Cross girls—Donut Dollies! They'll be flying in by chopper in three days."

Well, Miss America herself might as well have been coming. The news made the rounds of the base in less than an hour, apparently by far the most exciting thing to ever happen in Vung Ro Bay. The girls from the American Red Cross never came to our isolated bay way up in the mountains; there just weren't enough people there to warrant it, particularly as it involved so arduous a trip.

The base was in a state of exhilaration and anticipation, the news all anyone could discuss. It was a welcome distraction from the usual boredom.

"How many do you think are coming?" Johnny Dees asked me as we made our way to the dayroom for a strategy session. "Probably at least ten or twelve, huh?"

"Don't know, John. I sure hope so."

The soldiers stationed at Vung Ro Bay had not laid eyes on a 'round-eye' young woman ever since leaving the United States. For some, that meant close to a year. They were ecstatic over the prospect of real, live American girls coming to visit for a day.

Somehow, word had circulated through the base that twelve girls would be coming, just as Johnny Dees had suspected.

The strategy session produced some excellent ideas. The base would need to be spruced up as much as possible, everyone on the entire base pitching in. Old timbers would be removed from the side of the roads, bushes and wild shrubs would be cut down or trimmed, buildings would be cleaned up and painted if needed, sandbags straightened, trucks washed—whatever needed to be done to impress the young ladies from home.

Riggs was over in the corner of the dayroom, taking orders. He was going to make an emergency run to Tuy Hoa for cameras and film. This was one event that everyone wanted to have recorded. Time was of the essence. The dayroom was a hub of activity, full of representatives from all the diffcrent units on the base. There were stevedores from the 854th Transportation, truck drivers from the 545th, engineers from the 572 Engineer Company, firemen of the 520th, and radio techs from the 261st Signal Company. There must have been over a hundred of them. They all had ideas and input.

It was agreed that since there would be so many girls available that each unit in the bay would get two Dollies to take back to their respective compounds for a guided tour. That way, every company in the bay would have a chance to show off its area and explain their mission. The session was just about over; plans were made, and jobs were assigned to different people. Everyone was confident that the Red Cross girls would come away with a very good impression of Vung Ro Bay, their first-ever visit, and to a man, everyone present pledged to be on their best possible behavior, even Riggs. They all hoped that if things went well, it would assist in facilitating future visits.

Making my way to the bar to get another beer, I noticed Johnny Dees grinning. "What's so funny?"

"Can't tell you. You'll have to wait and see like everyone else."

Johnny Dees was not given to conversation just for conversation's sake. He was a quiet yet very likable young man. I knew that he had something big cooking in his brain. I noticed that Johnny sported a noticeable smirk the rest of the day. Something big was imminent, it seemed.

The next afternoon I returned from boat patrol and walked up towards the hootch when I spotted it. I stopped dead in my tracks. I had to look twice to make sure my eyes weren't playing tricks on me.

No, that's what it was, alright.

The only bathrooms in Vung Ro Bay were of the outhouse variety. Johnny Dees, the young MP, had realized that the young ladies might like to have a little more feminine style of restroom facility. In honor of the momentous event, he had mixed up some white paint with a little bit of red that he had borrowed from the Fire Department. He enlisted the assistance of Papa-San, the Vietnamese handyman, and created his masterpiece in just a few hours.

Papa-San painting the outhouse pink

The River Patrol Boat unit in Vung Ro Bay was the proud new owner of a pretty pink outhouse!

The day finally arrived. Vung Ro Bay had never looked so sharp. Someone even washed the PBR sign out in front of the compound. Everything was as neat as the GIs could get it. Of, course the mama-sans were a big help in cleaning everything up. They were there every day anyway, cleaning rooms and doing laundry, so it was natural for them to be brought into the project.

I chuckled when I saw that every man on base, including me, was dressed in uniform, as we were supposed to be. This is a first, I thought. We looked like an actual Army outfit.

A group of us were huddled around the dayroom, drinking beer and watching the skies. The early morning sun had just crested over the horizon of the South China Sea. It was a new day in Vietnam—and it was going to be a good one!

We stood around and waited. And waited. And waited some more. Beers kept appearing like magic from the dayroom refrigerator. A couple of hours later, the *whop-whop-whop* of a UH-1 Huey helicopter could be heard in the distance.

Helicopter with Red Cross girls arriving in Vung Ro Bay

"Here they come," yelled Kelly. "I can see a chopper!"

"How many choppers?" asked the NCOIC, already half-looped from getting started so early.

"One, Sarge. All I can see is one."

The chopper got closer and closer. Most of the soldiers on base had gathered near the landing pad. There must have been well over a hundred of them. Their mood began to change, however. They knew that one chopper was not a good sign.

"There can't be a dozen Red Cross girls on that bird," one of them observed.

"Hey guys," yelled Riggs, "Don't get too depressed. A Huey can carry eight, plus the crew. We've probably got at least half a dozen girls coming in!"

That was good news, and spirits rose once again, everyone very anxious for the arrival of the helicopter and the six beauties on board.

It touched down on the helo pad several minutes later amidst a swirl of dust and rotor noise. It was by far the most significant event ever to occur in Vung Ro Bay! The Beatles themselves couldn't have had a more enthusiastic crowd. Somebody wondered aloud if the perimeter bunkers were even being manned. Nobody knew, nor did they seem to care a whole lot at the moment.

The helicopter powered down, the rotors slowed, and the back door of the chopper slid open. Out jumped a door gunner. He had a broad smile on his face, realizing there were over a hundred soldiers who were jealous of his job at that moment.

"Why do they have the doors closed?" I asked no one in particular, "I don't think I've ever seen a Huey with its doors shut during flight."

"Probably to keep the girls' hair from getting messed up." offered Riggs.

The gunner reached back up and offered his hand to a young brunette dressed in the snappy blue uniform of the American Red Cross. A boisterous cheer arose. She looked bewildered for a moment, then smiled and waved at the small crowd. She had pale, white skin and a short light brown hairdo that flipped under at the end. Her perky, sincere smile displayed perfect white teeth, captivating everyone present.

The door gunner turned around and reached back up into the chopper and assisted another young girl, this one a short-haired blond, out of the aircraft, eliciting an even louder round of whoops and hollers from the group. She, too, smiled and waved with enthusiasm.

The soldiers of Vung Ro Bay were in heaven. All eyes turned back to the chopper. Who was next?

We all watched in horror as the door gunner reached up and slid the door of the helicopter closed. That's it? Only two girls! A sudden silence fell over the group, then someone came to their senses and started a round of applause. The girls beamed, waving to all as if in a parade back home on Main Street.

It didn't take long for everyone to adjust to the situation. We realized that two was much better than none. Two, as a matter of fact, was fine, just fine!

The base Commanding Officer, a Warrant Officer, greeted the young ladies and escorted them to the mess hall for lunch. It was just across the dirt road and up a slight incline from the helo pad.

The bunker guard from Kentucky was outside the mess hall, practicing as usual.

Thunk!... Thunk!... Thunk!

"Hey! One of you girls want to stand against this wall for me?"

The girls glanced at each other, giggled, and kept walking.

Fat Cook and the night baker had outdone themselves. They had managed to create a feast of grilled steaks, twice-baked potatoes, green beans, steamed carrots, fresh hot dinner rolls, and salad. He even had fresh water for cooking. We found out later that he had traded some things to a visiting freighter for water.

Fat Cook was beaming with pride as he placed a steak on my tray.

"Where the hell did you get steaks?"

"Well, they were part of a shipment destined for Tuy Hoa Air Base. Need I say more?"

"Nope."

Everyone ate well that day.

The two girls sat at a picnic table in the center of the room. The white linen tablecloths on every table did not go unnoticed by the two girls or by me, for that matter. Where in the world did Fat Cook come up with them? White tablecloths were unheard of in Vung Ro Bay.

Sometimes he surprised me.

Riggs had managed to get a seat on the bench right between the two young ladies. He had a stupid grin plastered on his face.

How the hell did he pull that off?

"There are close to 500 of us stationed here in Vietnam," I heard the blond say. "In case you guys don't know it, we sign up with the Red Cross right out of college and spend the same amount of time here as you do—one year. We usually spend most of our time at recreation centers on the larger bases, you know, helping soldiers write letters or coordinating games and activities. We spend quite a bit of time visiting wounded guys in the hospital, too. Because we stay so busy, our year passes a bit quicker."

"So, how did you get to come up here?" asked one of the young bunker guards.

"Well," the brunette answered, "Sometimes we get sent out in teams to base camps and isolated areas of Vietnam to provide whatever support we can offer. We'll travel by jeep, truck, or helicopter to get to where we need to go. I guess you guys just happened to be on a list somewhere."

"Yeah," said the blonde girl, "We were a bit apprehensive about coming up here. You guys are so isolated."

"You're safe here," said Riggs. "If we get hit, we'll just put you on a PBR and get out of Dodge!"

Both girls smiled.

The rest of the room was packed with young men wanting to know every little detail of what was happening back home and where they were from.

The girls smiled and did their best to answer everyone. They understood very well the loneliness the young men endured being so far away from home. I could tell that they were very well aware that all the young men around them appreciated their presence. I sat at a table, watching them. I wondered how they could smile so much. They never seemed to tire of the attention. They seemed to glow with that unique innocent charm that only American girls seem to possess. They were the quintessential girl next door.

Both had short hair due to the heat and humidity of Vietnam. Neither wore any makeup, just a slight hint of lipstick and, of course, perfume. The brunette was from Biloxi, Mississippi. Her name was Darlene. She had been in-country for almost a year, and this was her last visit to a remote base. She told us that the rest of her time would be spent at a Recreation Center in Saigon. I heard the other girl, the blond, say something about southern California. I would have to mention that to Kelly, the Los Angeles surfer.

After lunch, the two Red Cross girls made their way out of the mess hall and headed down to the PBR compound. Someone, probably Riggs, had let slip that the MPs over at the PBR compound had an inordinate amount of beer on hand.

The girls decided that it would be a good place to relax for a bit. Besides, the PBR compound was right on the beach.

The large Akai reel-to-reel tape deck—purchased with beer profits—was blaring out The Animal's *"We Gotta Get Out of This Place"* as they entered the dayroom. Both girls laughed and found seats at the end of the bar. The room was packed with GIs from the entire base. It was too crowded to play card games or anything else they would do at other bases to entertain troops. The guys just wanted to look at them.

After a couple of hours, Darlene mentioned that they would like to go down to the beach. She told several of her admirers that they had been visiting troops in the jungles of the Central Highlands for the past couple of weeks and couldn't wait to get in the ocean.

"I'm a beach girl," she told them. "I grew up in saltwater."

We led the girls out of the dayroom and down the sidewalk built just above the sand to the water's edge. It had been fabricated from wooden shipping pallets placed end to end. In anticipation of the girl's visit, the edges of the boards, about four inches on either end, had all been painted white.

Reaching the back of the Quonset hut, the girls spied the pink outhouse simultaneously, and both squealed with delight.

"That's fabulous!" the blond exclaimed. "Was that done for us?"

Riggs pointed to Johnny Dees.

"Oh! Thank you so much." The blond went over and gave him a quick peck on the cheek. "That's so thoughtful of you."

The boy from Ohio turned red as a beet.

I thought we might need to get the medic for a moment: Johnny Dees looked like he was on the verge of passing out!

The brunette, Darlene, walked down to the end of the wooden sidewalk and stepped onto the beach. She reached down, tossed her shoes off, and went right in—all the way up to her neck—still dressed in her Red Cross uniform. A couple of the PBR guys nearby jumped in with her and swam around several yards away.

I thought they looked a bit like sharks.

After a few minutes, the girls decided they needed their bathing suits to better enjoy the sun and beach. They had the foresight to pack them when they found out that they would be coming to a base with a beach.

Darlene, American Red Cross

McCall volunteered his room for them to change in, and they headed off towards the Quonset hut, passing the pink outhouse and giggling as they went.

It was getting late in the afternoon, and the crowd had thinned to perhaps 40 or 50 soldiers. Some had left to get back to work. Returning to the beach a few minutes later, the brunette, Darlene, turned up in a striking blue one-piece while the blonde was outfitted in a two-piece pink bikini.

You could have heard a pin drop—right there in the sand.

The Donut Dollies

The next morning, I woke up to just another regular day in Vung Ro Bay. The Red Cross girls had left the previous afternoon, and camp life was back to normal. Most of the base, I was sure, was in a state of severe depression. The excitement and delight of the girl's visit was over. It was time to get back to war.

I gathered up my shaving gear, soap dish, a change of clothes and walked out of my room. I passed the dayroom on my way to the shower. Memories of the previous days' activities came flooding back.

I tried not to look inside.

17. June 28, 1970

It was 9:00 a.m. on a lazy, quiet Sunday morning. Everyone was sleeping late, having been up later than usual for Riggs' 21st birthday party. The event carried on well into the early morning hours and was very well attended, not only by personnel of the 458th but also by members of various other units stationed at the Bay. Riggs was one of those people who seemed to make friends with everyone. He knew just about everyone at Vung Ro. It was a raucous party, enjoyed by all.

I had my feet up on the MP desk, chair tilted back, reading a recent copy of Road & Track magazine. Lee Beckman came strolling in the back door, looking like something the cat dragged in.

"What the hell are you doing in here?" he asked. "You're supposed to be out on patrol. Where's the boat?" Beckman was an E-5 and was the detachment maintenance supervisor. He was also the defacto NCOIC since the official one—the German guy—was drunk most of the time.

I explained that I had switched places with Johnny Dees that morning. He had been designated for desk duty that morning but hated just sitting there for twelve hours, doing nothing. He enjoyed operating the boats and had talked me into switching places with him at breakfast that morning. He would run the boat patrol, and I could sit and staff the MP Desk. It was the first and only time I'd ever switched places with anyone for duty.

PBR-32 approaching Echo Beach

"I don't know if that's such a good idea," Beckman said. "We've never had *all* MPs on the boat. That's definitely against every regulation there is!"

"Oh, come on, Lee. It's OK. What could possibly happen on a quiet Sunday morning?"

"How about Pearl Harbor?"

We both laughed and looked out the back door, seeing no sign of the PBR on patrol across the bay.

"OK, well, whatever. I guess it's done now," Beckman said as he started down the hallway, headed for the shower.

The sound of an explosion in the distance got my attention. I jumped up out of my chair at just about the same time that Beckman came running back in.

"What the hell was that?"

"Oh, they probably just threw a grenade on the beach," I replied. The crews liked to do that. It made a thunderous 'bang' like a cherry bomb on steroids. The trick was to get the PBR up to a good speed, run parallel to the beach as close in as possible, and have a crewman throw a concussion grenade on the shore. The boats could operate in only nine inches of water when 'up on step' at full speed, and the crews made a habit of practicing that maneuver whenever possible.

Dropping concussion grenade off Echo Beach

"I don't know," said Beckman. "I don't like this. We'd better find out what's going on."

Both of us went to the back door of the Quonset hut, stepped out onto the small landing at the top of the steps, and looked out across the bay. We could see smoke and a red flare coming from the direction of Foxtrot Beach. I turned and ran back inside to the radio.

"PBR 32, PBR 32, This is base, over."

"PBR 32. Come in. Come in!"

All I could hear was garbled static.

The crews at Vung Ro were all cross-trained to perform each other's duties when necessary. On this particular Sunday morning, the crew on PBR-32 was supposed to be two MP's from the 127th MP Company and one coxswain (me) from the 458th Transportation Company.

We had been to the east end of Bravo sector during the previous two days at about the same time each day when I was running the boat. On this Sunday morning, however, they returned once more.

The old wartime caution of "three on a match" being bad luck proved to be correct.

Beckman and I made several more attempts to raise the *Magic Christian* on the radio, but all we could get was static. Beckman grabbed a pair of binoculars.

"I can see them. There's a lot of smoke coming from the boat. There's another red flare! They're in big trouble."

"They've been hit!" Beckman yelled. "Go get everybody up!"

I ran to the hootch barracks next door to alert the rest of the detachment.

"They've been hit!" I yelled as I stormed into the hootch, waking everyone up with a sudden jolt. "Get up, you guys. 32 has been hit!"

Everyone bounded out of their bunks and scrambled into their clothes. They grabbed their weapons and hurried out of the building.

I ran back to the radio room. Beckman was on the phone with the Vung Ro Control Center, located up on the hill, to report the incident, as was required by protocol.

McCall and three others ran down to the docks, cast off the lines, and took off in the other PBR. They ripped the canvas covers off the guns and then threw them on the deck, the .50-calibers spitting fire in the direction of the cove.

McCall and the crew of *Captain America* arrived on the scene after briefly strafing the cove with machine gun fire. McCall told us later he was ready to pull up alongside if need be and take the stricken PBR in tow. He said he had yelled over at Dees and asked him if he needed to be towed, but he said Dees looked at him through bloodied eyes and waved him off. He said Dees had blood covering the top of his head but seemed to be coherent enough to run the boat. The damaged boat then continued towards our dock.

PBR 'Captain America' firing into the cove

About a half-hour later, as the PBR got closer, the damage became evident. Everyone ran down to the docks to help them land. Guards who witnessed the event from their perimeter bunkers scrambled down their ladders and rushed to the dock to assist. It seemed to take forever to get the boat in. They were just about abreast of the pier when, to add to the drama, a huge landing craft, an LST, was about to make a landing on the beach next to the docks. The PBR slowly continued on its course to safety, oblivious to the presence of the landing ship. The skipper of the landing ship sounded the danger signal of five blasts on the horn, but the little PBR paid no attention. Dees kept pointing the PBR toward the safety of the pier. All of us on the dock were yelling and waving our arms, trying to alert him of the impending disaster. Dees paid no attention to anyone—he just kept coming. The LST almost plowed into them, missing the patrol boat by less than fifty feet. Several of the ship's crew were peering down over the gunwales, stunned at the sight of the destroyed patrol boat.

LST ship that had narrowly missed crashing into PBR

Beckman was standing on the dock, having called the base Control Center again for a medic, telling them that men had been wounded. The boat was very close to the pier, and one of the MP's aboard, Rich Morgan, looked like he wanted to jump. When the boat got closer to the dock, he did just that. He took a flying leap across the two or three-foot gap separating the boat from the dock and collapsed on top of Beckman. Beckman took his arm, put it around his neck, and hoisted him to his feet. Others rushed up to help as the damaged PBR crashed into the pier, almost knocking everyone off their feet.

Bow damage from a rocket-propelled grenade (RPG)

"Get lines secured to that boat!" yelled Beckman.

The base medic, Doc Webster, came running down the beach and scrambled onto the dock. He jumped aboard the boat carrying his medic bag.

"You guys all sit down and let me have a look at you," he said to the crew as he motioned to the engine hatches.

Not one of them said a word. All were in a state of shock and disbelief. The rest of us all just stood there, staring at the wounded crew and the destroyed boat. It was the first time the war had hit that close to home.

"Damn. It looks like a B-40 rocket got 'em," said Young. "Nothing else would do that kind of damage."

"I heard it coming!" Dees yelled. "I just didn't know what it was."

"OK, let's get these guys up closer to the helo pad," said the medic. "They all need to get medevac'd."

Force of explosion split ½" steel tub back plate

Beckman and an MP started walking Morgan up to the dayroom. He was going into shock from the explosion and was only semi-conscious. Beckman took him up to the area outside of the dayroom, laid him down, and the medic treated him for shock. He elevated his feet, put him on a stretcher, and covered him with a blanket. Johnny Dees and Kelly were both bloodied, having been hit with shrapnel from the exploding steel surrounding the gun tub and from other areas of the bow.

"I heard the damn thing coming!" Dees yelled again to no one in particular. "I just didn't know what it was."

Doc Webster tried to make them as comfortable as possible as they waited for the medevac chopper Base Control had called in. He changed the bandages on Kelly's head as his wound seemed to be the worst. Johnny Dees just sat in a lounge chair, holding the application on his head.

The NCOIC pulled up a chair. "You know I've got to make a report, Johnny. What the hell happened out there?"

The NCOIC and Johnny Dees sat in the corner of the dayroom, Dees recounting the events and the NCOIC writing down as much as he could.

Shortly thereafter, the *whop-whop-whop* of a Medevac chopper could be heard in the distance.

"OK, Sarge, we gotta go." yelled the medic. "Chopper's coming in."

"Alright, Johnny. We'll have to finish this up when you get back," said the NCOIC. "Go ahead on out to the chopper."

Medical Evacuation helicopter

Doc Webster helped Beckman carry Morgan over to the Huey and loaded him in as gently as possible. Beckman had covered Morgan's head with a blanket so sand from the helicopter downdraft wouldn't blow in his face. He looked up to see a look of sadness on the co-pilot's face. Uncovering his face briefly, Beckman told him, "Don't worry, he ain't dead. He's in shock."

Johnny Dees and Kelly were able to get on the chopper unassisted. Then they lifted off and were gone.

"I wonder what happened out there?" I said to Beckman on the way back to the dayroom."

"Looks like they were in the wrong place at the wrong time," he answered. "Had to be a B-40, though."

Entry point of RPG

The base Command Center had notified the Korean White Horse Division stationed on the bluff high above Vung Ro Bay. They began firing on the cove with 105mm Howitzer cannons, potentially obliterating anything or anyone still in the area.

After the crew had been medevac'd, the rest of the PBR contingent and many men from other units converged on the pier and the beach.

"Wow, I can't believe they made it back!" said Young. "I've never seen a boat with that much damage still float."

Destroyed bow of PBR 'Magic Christian'

Beckman noticed that I had become reticent.

"What's up, 32?" he asked.

"Well, I was just thinking that I might have just missed an appointment with death. I was on that boat the last two days, and we went to the cove fishing. If I'd been on it today, we'd have gone back there again. I'd have been a lot closer to the shore than Johnny was since I knew the waters better. There probably wouldn't be a boat left."

"OK, let's start getting the guns and whatever else we can get," said the NCOIC. "It still might sink right here at the dock."

Beckman and I boarded the craft and made our way to the bow. "Oh man," I said. "This is really bad. I almost feel like crying. I'm so glad those guys are OK, but I've put so much work into this boat. I can't believe it's destroyed!"

"Yeah, well, at least they're all alive," Beckman said.

The Chief showed up on the scene, boarded the boat, and went to the aft .50 caliber machine gun. He removed it from its mount and started off to the cleaning tub on shore.

"I can't believe he carries those things all by himself," I said. "I always have to remove the barrel first."

"Yeah, he likes to show off," replied Beckman.

"He's so weird. Why doesn't he ever go out on patrol? He's an MP, but all he ever does is hang around in his room or sit on that damn rock down by the beach. And every time Riggs goes to the Air Base, the Chief is with him. He sure as hell doesn't pull his share of the work around here."

"Well, he's only got a short time left," said Beckman. "Also, I heard that he's got something on the NCOIC. I think it's something bad—like a court-martial offense, you know?"

"Oh well, that would explain a lot. I wonder what the Sarge did."

"I don't know, but I heard it was from when they were both in Qui Nhon together. As much as the Sarge drinks, it could have been anything."

"Yeah, and I think he gets Riggs to stop at one of the little 'pot shops' on the way to town. That's probably why he wears those stupid sunglasses all the time—so we can't see his glassy eyes!"

"You're probably right. Wouldn't surprise me a bit."

We finished removing all we could from the boat when a bulldozer showed up on the beach.

"OK, Three-two. Go ahead and fire it up and move her around to the beach." yelled the NCOIC. "We've got to get it out of the water."

Beckman and I untied the lines, slowly motored around to the other side of the dock, and nosed the boat onto the beach sand. A couple of others hooked up cables to the bow cleats and the dozer pulled the destroyed boat up onto the sand.

Destroyed PBR 32 on the beach

Later that afternoon, I was standing on the small landing just outside the RTO room. It was a quiet, calm, and serene afternoon. There was no noise to be heard anywhere.

Strange.

I walked down the steps and jumped off the concrete pad that formed the rear of our company area. The beach was soft. I kicked off my flip-flops and started walking towards the Delong pier.

Before I realized it, I was standing directly in front of the Chief's rock. I looked the rock over. The chunks of coral and whatever else it was composed of had been worn down from centuries of relentless surf.

It had a very inviting look, though.

The Chief's Rock

I climbed up into the rock and rested my back against the curvature. It was quite comfortable. The tide was almost at its highest point, and every so often, a wave would splash against the base, sending a spray of water cascading up into the air and covering the rock in a fine sea mist. I began to understand what the Chief saw in this old rock sitting on the beach all by itself. There was nothing like this back in his home of Arizona.

A strange feeling came over me sitting on that rock. Maybe by imagination, maybe by osmosis, I don't know, but somehow, I felt a connection. The rock held secrets—secrets of the French colonialists, secrets of the Viet Cong, secrets of the newly-arrived Americans, secrets of the Apache even.

A feeling of peace swelled within me. At that very moment, everything was just fine. The war was fine. My being away from home was fine. Even the Viet Cong were fine.

.

Morgan and Johnny Dees returned to duty at Vung Ro Bay several days later, Dees suffered a blown eardrum, and Morgan had the top of his ear torn off completely, and both suffered multiple shrapnel wounds. Kelly never returned. He only had eight days left in-country and had been sent down to Saigon to wait out the rest of his time. They sent someone to retrieve all of his personal possessions.

The entire base was aware of the return of the two PBR crewmen. The dayroom that night became the domain of Johnny Dees. He had usurped the throne from Riggs, at least for one night. Dees sat at the bar with Morgan, beers at hand. The entire dayroom was filled to capacity with men from most of the units in the bay. It was standing room only.

"OK, OK, settle down, everyone," yelled Riggs. "Go ahead, Johnny."

Dees sheepishly began his story, aware of a hundred eyes staring at him. "Well," he began, "When we left here, we ran out into the ocean a little bit, then decided to head over to the far side of the bay. I ran the boat up to its full speed of around thirty-five knots on the way over."

"Yeah," added Morgan. "We were just enjoying watching the water splash off the sides of the bow and listening to the deep, throaty roar of those twin diesels."

"So," Dees continued, "the boat was 'in trim' and barreling along, just skimming the top of the water. We were having a blast. As we approached the area of Echo Beach, I eased back on the throttles. As the boat slowed, I made my approach to the rocky outcrop just between Echo Beach and Foxtrot Beach. Morgan and Kelly had been out there on Friday and Saturday with Hebert. We figured since fishing was so good in that area, we could drop a concussion grenade or two and have a good haul of fish for Sunday dinner."

The dayroom was quieter than it had ever been. All were engrossed in Dee's story.

"So, I had the boat parallel to the shore, running about five knots. We were close enough that I could easily have thrown a rock and hit the beach. Then, without any warning, the entire bow of the boat just jumped up out of the water. For a split-second, I thought I ran aground on a sandbar, and then I realized that there had been an immense explosion."

"Yeah, we heard it all the way back here," said one of the bunker guards.

"The explosion was the loudest thing I've ever heard. My ears were ringing so bad I couldn't hear a damn thing, and then my eyes watered up real bad. I felt like I was in a daze. It was almost like a dream, to be honest. I kinda came to a bit, then realized we had to get the hell out of there, so I threw both throttles full forward. I remember trying to look at the gauges on the control panel, but all I could see was blood. I used one hand to feel around and see where it was coming from. I figured out it was coming from my head. I had to force myself to remain calm so that I could stay in control of the situation. I tried so hard to remember everything Hebert had taught me."

"Well, it looks like you were a pretty good instructor, Three-two," the NCOIC interjected.

At this point, many of the attendees needed another beer, so we all took a five-minute break, refreshed our beverages, and then returned to our seats.

"As I was bringing the boat up to speed, I regained some of my hearing and heard one of the MPs yelling. I turned around to see Kelly standing on the stern pointing at Morgan, floating in the water some fifty or sixty meters behind us."

Everybody stared at Morgan.

"Anyway, he had been blown overboard! So, I cranked the wheel hard starboard and slammed the right throttle into reverse without letting off on the speed. The reverse gate dropped over the outlet on the starboard jet drive and skidded the boat around in its own length, just like Three-two had shown me. I spun the steering wheel back to midships, slammed the right throttle forward, and sped back to where Morgan was."

"Weren't you worried about getting shot at?" someone asked.

"Of course, but there was nothing I could do. I couldn't leave Morgan there to swim to shore. They might have taken him prisoner."

"Yeah, and then I'd have really been pissed!" added Morgan, as the room broke into laughter.

"As we got close to Morgan, I yelled at Kelly to strafe the shore with .50 caliber fire. I was hoping the gooks were already making their way out of the area and wouldn't attack us again. When we got close to Morgan, I slowed headway and pulled up alongside him. He was bloody but conscious and treading water."

Morgan raised his beer in triumph. Cheers erupted from the crowd.

"I got close enough to him so that Kelly could reach over the side and grab him under the arms and haul him back in, just the way they pick up Navy Seals during special ops."

"Yeah, but I ain't no Navy Seal," yelled Morgan. "That hurt like hell."

More laughter from the crowd.

"After Kelly got Morgan on board, he just slumped on the deck like a bag of rags. He kept asking what happened, over and over."

"And I couldn't hear a word you were saying," Morgan added. "My hearing was shot to hell."

"Yeah, finally, I yelled that it had been an RPG, probably a B-40. I remember seeing the black smoke trail. I remember the first thing you said, Morgan. You looked at the bow and said that was where you were supposed to be sitting."

"Is that luck, or what?" Morgan smiled.

"So, after we got Morgan back on board, I jammed both throttles full ahead and put the beach to my stern while Kelly fired off a red flare and then tended to Morgan's wounds. He was bleeding, but Kelly couldn't find anything severe, so he told him to lie down on the engine hatch and rest.

"I had a hard time looking out through the canvas covering the coxswain's flat. Either blood or tears filled my eyes. I don't know which. I could see the base far off in the distance. It looked so far away, and the boat was moving so slowly. I remember thinking that something just didn't feel right. The boat felt sluggish and wasn't getting "up on step" like it was supposed to. From the coxswain's flat, I could see a considerable amount of damage to the forward .50-caliber gun tub, and it looked like part of the bow had been blown away. I was thankful that both the guys had been in the stern getting ready for fishing. Had Morgan been sitting in that gun tub, he would have been mangled beyond recognition."

Everyone looked at Morgan again. He smiled.

"You know, if that gook had fired his rocket a mere one or two seconds later, it would have hit amidships, right where we all were. We would all be dead. I can't believe how lucky we are."

"Yeah, boats can be replaced," I said.

"Anyway," Dees continued. "I could tell that something wasn't right, so I yelled to Kelly to go below and have a look. He came back up less than a minute later and said we were taking on a lot of water through a big gash in the bow. I asked him to turn the bilge pump on, but he said there was no way it could handle it. There was too much water coming in."

"What did you do?" one of the stevedores asked.

"Wait just a second. I'm getting to that."

"Oh, OK."

"So, I couldn't figure out what to do. I knew we were a long way from the base and would probably sink before we got there. I guess I was in a panic, sort of. I remember thinking that we were alone. Alone, defeated, and scared. It was so quiet too. Even with the roar of the diesels, it just seemed so quiet."

"Yeah, I was layin' on the deck, and I heard him yell for us to get our life jackets on," said Morgan. "Kelly went below and brought them up and helped me get into mine."

"So, the water was pouring into the bow, and I had the boat planed out a little. Then Kelly yells at me to slow it down some and see if the bow would rise up any. I reached for both throttles, brought them back to about 1000 RPMs, and sure enough, the bow came up as the stern sank a bit. I told Kelly to go below and check the bow. He came back up and said the water had slowed to a manageable stream. The bilge pump was going like mad."

"You guys are sure lucky, I'll say that," said Beckman. "That was a good idea to slow it down and let the bow rise up a bit."

"Yeah, we stayed at that speed, then I saw McCall coming towards us in the 29 boat. He wanted to take us in tow, but I thought we could make it OK."

"Well, you were right. You did good, Johnny." Said McCall.

"I just tried to remember everything you guys had taught me," Dees answered.

"This is unbelievable!" someone muttered.

"Yeah, that's just what I was thinking—all the way back.

Entry point of B-40 rocket

A few days later, we found out from the NCOIC that the Purple Heart medal had been awarded to all three.

Everyone in the PBR detachment thought Dees, however, should be awarded a Bronze Star for heroism. The NCOIC agreed and started filling out the necessary paperwork needed to begin processing the request.

"You know," Beckman reminded the NCOIC. "Questions might be raised that can't be answered. Why was a patrol sent out with only MPs and no coxswain? And why was Hebert not on board?"

The NCOIC stopped writing, looked at Beckman for a moment, then tore the paperwork in half and threw it in the wastebasket.

■

I found Johnny Dees sitting in the dayroom, nursing a beer. "What's up, Johnny?"

"Not much. Just thankful to be alive. And I'm starting to get worried."

"About what?"

"Well, for one thing, I'm worried about how HQ is going to handle this. There was no coxswain on that boat, just a bunch of MPs. How the hell are we going to explain that? We're probably both facing a court-martial, you know?"

"Yeah," I answered. "You're probably right. Maybe we'll get to be cellmates, though."

"God, I can't believe you can make a joke at a time like this!"

Johnny Dees and I waited and waited for our orders to report to Saigon and thence, no doubt, the U.S. military stockade: Long Binh Jail. It never happened. Nothing more was ever heard officially about the event.

The NCOIC had plenty of flaws, without a doubt, but nobody could dispute the fact that he took care of his boys.

The *Magic Christian* sat on the beach for several days, a stark reminder of the dangers of war. A few days later, an LCU from Qui Nhon arrived to pick it up. A bulldozer and a large wheeled forklift finally managed to get it loaded in the well deck of the landing craft. It was the last I ever saw of my boat.

18. Looking for Charlie

Later that day, my crew and I were on patrol near the entrance to the bay. Our unit was now down to only one boat, so shifts had to share the *Captain America*.

Two jets from the 31st Tactical Air Wing at Tuy Hoa Air Force Base flew in low and fast several hours after the attack on PBR-32 and spent the better part of an hour saturating the north end of Vung Ro Bay with napalm and 500-pound bombs.

U.S. Air Force jets dropping bombs into the cove

If anyone had been notified of the incoming airstrike, the information never made it down as far as me. The sudden

"Whoosh!" scared me to death as the fighter jets came screaming in over our heads under cover of darkness. Then the sky lit up in a blaze of thunder and light.

We brought our boat to a stop just off the beach at Echo Point and drifted, watching the entire north end of the bay explode into rolling walls of flames as the napalm hit the ground. All I could do was stare at the spectacle before me. I had never been this close to an airstrike before; I had never even seen an airstrike before. I was horrified by the sight, yet somehow it fascinated me. Smoke hung in dense low clouds all around the bay.

"It sure took them a while to get here," I muttered. "The attack was this morning."

"Maybe they had another mission," yelled Young. "Too bad we couldn't have had these guys here for the 4th of July."

•

The break of dawn brought a Korean White Horse Division unit down to the bay from their perch high atop the mountain. Their mission was to sweep the previous night's bombing areas and retrieve any bodies or weapons. They arrived in two deuce-and-a-half trucks and proceeded to the concrete ramp. A landing craft was waiting from the 1099th Medium Boat Company, whose job was to transport the Korean team into the cove and return them to the base after the mission.

The 458th Sea Tigers were tasked with providing escort, cover, and fire support for the search and destroy mission, not that there would be much left to destroy. Another PBR had been sent down overnight from Qui Nhon to replace the destroyed *Magic Christian,* but it was a real clunker. It had been run hard with little maintenance or care.

McCall and his crew waited at the dock. The LCM was nosed up to the beach not 100 feet away while the Koreans began offloading from their trucks. They were all dressed in full combat gear as they marched onto the landing craft, none uttering a single word. They all squeezed in close together to allow as many men as possible on the well deck. Some of the sergeants and officers made their way to the aft deck and stood behind the wheelhouse.

I had gathered up my crew, and we cast off from the dock ahead of the assault party. We made our way to the sweep area and 'softened up' things with our .50 caliber machine guns.

Landing Craft (LCM-8) waiting for Korean troops

"Fire up along the ridgeline," Beckmann yelled to the MP on the aft machine gun. "Shooting along the beach is useless."

A few minutes later, we heard the unmistakable sound of a Huey gunship coming right over our heads. They had also been sent to shoot up the area prior to the Korean landing. I turned the replacement PBR away from the beach just in time to get inundated with the hot, empty shells that the helicopters' miniguns were discharging. They were raining down all over us, bouncing off the top of the canopy and flying all around. The two MPs scrambled from their machine guns and took cover under the canvas top of the coxswain flat.

"This is ridiculous," said Beckman. "Let's back off a bit. I think these guys can handle things from here."

I put the boat in gear, and we sped off, passing the other PBR and the LCM loaded with Koreans. We took up a position behind the LCM and followed them. A short time later, they arrived at the end of the cove, beaching the LCM on a narrow, sandy strip. Someone fired a canister of red smoke, allowing the troops to determine wind direction.

PBR 'Captain America' providing cover support

The Koreans piled off the LCM as quietly as they had arrived. They were a well-disciplined, no-nonsense, take-no-prisoners type of unit. The Viet Cong feared them. They thought nothing of decapitating a prisoner and leaving his head as a warning to others.

The sweep lasted for several hours, resulting in nothing of note. Anyone who had been unlucky enough to have been around the previous night was no longer in existence. The Koreans concluded that the enemy had departed the scene immediately after the attack on the patrol boat, which made sense, as the Viet Cong favored hit and run tactics.

"Those Korean guys looked a bit disappointed when they got back on the LCM," McCall told me later in the dayroom.

"Yeah, I guess they couldn't chop off any heads today," quipped Rinslow, his aft .50 caliber gunner, who was sitting nearby.

■

Shortly after this bit of excitement, the compound was in an uproar over wild speculation after an abrupt departure by the German and the arrival of a new NCOIC, a Military Police Sergeant First Class from CID, which worried us.

Several of us were gathered around in the dayroom. "Why in the world would they send someone from Criminal Investigations down to oversee us?" I asked. "Are they checking on our excessive ammunition usage?"

"I dunno," said Beckman. "Maybe they found out about the all-MP crew on the boat that got blown up, or maybe they found out about the stolen beer. Hell, it could be any number of things."

There were so many questions, and for the next several days, we were all on our very best behavior. We had to figure this guy out. His name was Caleb Brown, and he sported a very military-style crew cut. He said he had been sent down from Qui Nhon to replace the drunk. Eventually, after several weeks had passed, we figured out that he would fit in just fine. He seemed unaware of the hijinks we had all been involved in. Being assigned to Vung Ro Bay was probably just a vacation for him.

We had previously kept all weapons in the arms room. SFC Brown initiated a new system immediately upon his arrival.

"This is a war zone," he declared. "Weapons need to be with you at all times."

From then on, everyone kept a gun in their room, close at hand. Beckman and the other engineer, Tommy Young, shared a room in the Quonset addition. Young chose an M-16 and hung it off the end of his top bunk. Beckman had his .45-caliber pistol hung next to his head. A machete safely tucked away hanging down through the floorboards was within easy reach if needed. Beckman didn't think much of Young having an M-16 in the room. Charlie had a habit of infiltrating the perimeter and killing whoever they could find. Beckman was determined not to have that happen to him. A pistol and machete were much better in close combat than an M-16, he reckoned.

.

My sleep was interrupted just after midnight by loud and frequent explosions, lots of them, one after another, in rapid succession. The sound was deafening. We were all jarred awake and ran to the dayroom as debris came raining down on the tin roof of our Quonset hut. Material from high up on the hill could be heard splashing into the water, close to shore. We all knew right away what had happened: the gooks had finally gotten Bunker 11. The large fortress-like guard tower rested on a high cliff overlooking the sea on one side and Vung Ro Bay on the other. Its sheer size and location defined it as impregnable. It was built better than any of the others and was protected by claymores, a .50-caliber machine gun, and searchlights.

Bunker 11 had been successful in withstanding at least two previous B-40 rocket attacks.

In the distance, I could hear the bursts of heavy machine-gun fire coming from one of the PBR's on night patrol. I grabbed my M-16 and ran out into the night. Signal flares burst forth from the remaining perimeter bunkers and lit up the night sky. The entire base came to life.

Riggs appeared next to me. "What the hell?"

"It looks like they finally got Bunker 11."

Bunker 11
(Before, with visible evidence of two B-40 rocket attacks)

I ran into the hallway of the Quonset addition to make sure everyone was up. The door to Beckman's room was open.

Young had bailed out of his bunk first and was in the doorway, firing away from the prone position. Beckman tried climbing out of his bunk, but his pistol belt got hung up on the back of his mattress, causing him to fall out onto the floor with the bed on top of him. Young was firing madly, and the empty cartridges were bouncing off the wall and back at Beckman. Deciding that being hunkered down under a mattress wasn't such a bad place to be, Beckman settled in.

I made sure I was out of the way. "Hey!" I yelled.

"What the hell are you doing?" yelled Young, looking over at Beckman.

"Being shielded from your empty shells landing on top of me. I'll come out when it's safe. What are you trying to do?"

"The gooks are inside the wire! I've got to shoot that light out over on the pier by bunker 12. There's too much light on the road!"

Beckman couldn't quite see the logic in that. Young never accomplished his task.

The three of us hurried outside to gaze up at the hilltop, once the domain of an imposing, powerfully defended defensive tower. Columns of thick, black smoke wafted up into the placid night sky. We saw a large bed of burning embers—sparks twinkling up into a dark night sky. The sappers had obliterated every trace of the giant, impenetrable bunker.

"Yeah. Look, there's a bunch of guys over at the mess hall. Let's go see what's up." Beckman said.

We walked in just in time to hear a young soldier yelling. "I was just up there, not 5 minutes ago," he cried. "Wes and I did a rock-paper-scissors to see which one of us would hike down here and pick up some chow. Now he's dead."

The young GI started to shake and burst into tears just as the medic arrived and led him away.

"I was just up there. I was just up there. Oh God, this is all my fault," he whimpered. "I should have been there."

"Where's he taking him?" I asked.

"Oh, probably back to the medic shack. He's going to need a shot of something and some rest." Beckman answered.

"They're going to have to medevac him outta here," I said. "He won't ever be able to stand bunker duty again."

Young, Beckman, and I made our way to the 458th bunker and took refuge with several others. Someone had set up a radio in the bunker, and one of the PBRs soon radioed in that they needed .50-caliber ammo. "I'll go down and do it," Beckman volunteered. "Tell them I'll carry it down and set it on the dock, and the boat can just nose in and pick it up."

He had gone to the PBR bunker in a helmet, flak jacket, and no shoes. He made one trip from the ammo bunker to the dock carrying the heavy ammo box barefoot. On the way back up, he stopped by his room, removed his helmet and flak vest, and put on a pair of boots. It was much easier to carry the ammo boxes after that.

On one of Beckman's return trips, he stopped by the dayroom for a drink of water and found Young and several others that he did not know. They were from the bunker guard company and a couple of other units on the base.

"What are you guys up to?"

"We're organizing a party to retake Bunker 11 and the hill," Young replied. Even though his regular job was as an engineer on a PBR, he knew this was an important event.

Several in attendance began strapping on extra ammo and filling canteens from the yucky water cooler.

"Are you guys crazy?" I asked.

"It's got to be done," Young answered, as others checked their weapons. "If the gooks get control of that hilltop, we're all dead meat. They can just sit up there and take us all out, one by one."

Beckman continued to carry ammo boxes down to the dock while Young and his group departed for the mission up the hill. Rinslow had decided to join the patrol at the last minute.

"How are we going up there?" Rinslow asked one of the bunker guards.

"We'll go around the back of the mess hall and take the road up. It'll take too much time, and it's too hard to climb the hill. Just be on your guard. There's no telling how many Viet Cong are up there."

Beckman and I stood on the roadway outside the compound and watched Young and his group carefully make their way up the road.

Later that night, Young and Rinslow held court in the dayroom, telling their story.

"We arrived at the bunker site without incident. I guess the enemy had already disappeared into the shelter of the night." Young started.

"You guys wouldn't have believed it," Rinslow added. "There was nothing left—I mean *nothing!*"

"We got up there and found the place leveled," said Young. "It was obvious the bunker guard had been blown to bits. One of the other guys who went up with us even started to cry when he saw the destruction. I'll tell you guys; I've never seen anything like it. I mean, that bunker was three stories high and damn well impregnable. The gooks must have been around the base of it for quite some time setting all the satchel charges. The poor guard never even knew they were down there."

"So, the other guard who came down for chow must have walked right by them," I said.

"Did you find him?" asked Beckman.

"I think we found pieces of him," Young replied. "His name was Wesley, I believe."

Young standing at Bunker 11 (after)

■

Boredom is not the right word to describe the mood that struck the men of the 458th on occasion. Maybe 'total lack of activity' would be a better term. When there were no ships in port, and if the Viet Cong weren't attacking, there wasn't very much for them to do. The base was very small. Everybody had explored every inch of it many times over.

Riggs, Rinslow, Johnny Dees, and I were sitting in the dayroom, looking at the tacky red, white, and blue plastic streamers hanging along the entire length of the room.

"Who hung that stupid stuff up there?" Dees asked.

"Someone must have had it sent to them a long time ago," Riggs volunteered. "It's been up as long as I've been here. I'm surprised the thumbtacks haven't rusted through yet." They all mumbled agreement, acknowledging the tacky decoration of their dayroom. Nobody, however, ever attempted to do anything about it.

Dees put his can of Olympia beer down on the bar and sighed. "Something's got to give. I'm going stir-crazy!"

"How about we all go into Tuy Hoa tomorrow? I'm sure we can find something to do there," offered Riggs.

"Naw. We've seen all the movies. There won't be any new ones coming in until sometime next week. There's just nothing at all to do."

Rinslow, who until this point had been engrossed in a James Michener novel, piped up out of the blue.

"They had a dust-off mission up on the mountain last night. There were Huey gunships all over the place. They were shooting all over the mountainside. Why don't we do a recon patrol and see if we can find any bodies? We can hike up to Signal Mountain while we're at it. I've never been up there."

All at once, everyone's face lit up. At last, adventure! Signal Mountain was up at the top of Vung Ro Mountain. It was a long, very steep climb—at least three or four miles. It would take them the better part of the day to get up there and back on foot.

"Yeah, that's a great idea," added Johnny Dees. "We might be able to get a few AK-47's for souvenirs."

We planned the reconnaissance patrol for the next day. All of us spent the rest of that afternoon getting weapons cleaned, making sure canteens of water were filled, and trying to talk several others into joining 'The Mission.' Although several expressed interest, everybody else either had to go out on boat patrol or had better things to do.

The little group assembled in front of the dayroom, some dressed in fatigue pants with no shirt, another in cutoff shorts and a fatigue shirt. We all wore flip-flops. We slung our M-16's over our shoulders and started out. Our flak jackets, helmets, and boots remained where they were: in our lockers.

"Hey!"

We stopped and turned to see who was hailing us.

"Where are you guys going?" inquired Beckman.

"Recon mission," answered Dees. "Going up to Signal Mountain."

"Not without me, you're not." He turned and hurried off towards his room. "Wait right there."

No one had thought to invite Beckman. He was in a sort of limbo status. By virtue of his rank, he was technically an NCO, but then, on the other hand, he was also one of the guys. He was, however, invited to the events of mayhem more often than not.

Returning a few minutes later, Beckman joined the group, and we all marched up the dirt road past the lumber yard, heading for the perimeter. Again, being the only one with any sense, Beckman came prepared with his flak jacket, combat boots, an M-16, a .45-caliber pistol, and his ever-present machete. The helmet, however, didn't make it.

Trekking up the rocky dirt road, we encountered a perimeter bunker guard climbing down the ladder from his bunker. "What are you guys doin?"

"Recon patrol," smiled Beckman. "The choppers last night must have hit something. We're going to find out what."

"Shouldn't you leave that to the Koreans?" asked the bunker guard.

No one answered. We headed up the hill.

∎

We had been hiking for close to an hour when, under a canopy of dead tree limbs, we stumbled upon the remnants of the Old French Fort, long the subject of discussion and rumor in Vung Ro but never visited by anyone.

Our "Recon Squad" arrived at the site of the battle shortly before lunchtime. We walked halfway down the dirt road and passed through two old rock columns, standing at attention in the dazzling blue summer sky. They were but sentinels to a lost cause.

The Viet Cong had annihilated the forces at the French Fort, midway up Vung Ro Mountain, sometime in the 1950s. Nothing much remained save for the occasional sandbagged bunker or outbuilding. Most of the fort was enclosed with a stone wall, jagged, cracked, and shattered from many years of weather and neglect—the narrow, broken trees cast half-hearted shadows across the barren, lonely landscape.

"They say that over 1100 French soldiers were killed here when the 'Cong overran this place," announced Riggs. "That must have been a helluva fight."

"The Koreans won't even come here on patrol," added Beckman. "They're terrified of the long-dormant ghosts and spirits that awaken and haunt the place. Sergeant ROK told me that passing by here late at night, they can hear voices—sometimes whimpering and sobbing—the lost souls of the French soldiers who were massacred here."

"I've heard that birds won't even land here," Riggs said. "They make a wide detour around the place."

I listened with great interest. Since it was my first visit to the once-proud stronghold of the French Army, I was not surprised that the fort did indeed have an eerie, ghostly feel to it. Having never stood on the site of a massacre before, I had the feeling of being on hallowed ground, standing in the midst of the dead. I felt like an invader, as if I had no right to be there.

We decided to have lunch at the fort, which consisted of nothing more than a few cans of C-rations.

Maybe we might hear something.

The old French Fort at Vung Ro Bay

After a hasty meal, I wandered over and studied the heavily-weathered old worn rock walls. The French had controlled Vietnam for a hundred years, and this fort was a magnificent structure, desolate as it was. The workmanship, even in its dilapidated state, was impeccable. Every stone had been cut with precision and placed in just the proper spot. It was evident that it had been constructed by skilled craftsmen, men who had patience and plenty of time—French craftsmen. It looked like they had visions of building a small palace or something, a structure worthy of Parisian artisans.

I glanced out over the jagged rock formations protecting the fort from the seaside. We were up on a wind-blown cliff top. The view was incredible, and I could see for miles. In the distance, the glistening South China Sea spread an expansive, sweeping vista across an infinite horizon. The mournful and mysterious fort possessed a hidden beauty unrivaled in the Central Coast of Vietnam.

"This must have been a hell of a fort back in the old days." I said.

No one heard me.

The knowledge of the events that had occurred there captivated me and caused a great feeling of sadness. One thousand one hundred brave, courageous young men. What must they have been thinking as they watched wave after wave of raging Viet Cong scale the walls of the fort? Did they realize they were all going to die? I imagined the fear—the horror—they must have felt.

It was a depressing and empty place. The dead seemed to be crying from the perfectly-carved, wind-blown rocks and stones. I walked slowly down a narrow, rock-lined pathway, eerily leading the way to nowhere. The elephant grass surrounding the perimeter swayed gently against the sea breeze, whispering the secrets of the horrible massacre.

Evidence of human misery was everywhere. Those poor young soldiers, soldiers just like me, would never return home to tell stories of their service in Vietnam. They would never go home. They would never stare in awe at the magnificence of the Eiffel Tower lit up at night. They would never sit by the banks of the Seine with a baguette and a bottle of red. They would never clutch the hand of a beautiful young girl as they strolled down the Champs-Élysées on a starry summer night. They would never again see a sunrise. They would never again see a sunset. They would never do anything, ever again. Their stories were gone—to remain forever untold.

I could feel a lump start to grow in my throat.

I felt the trace of a tear trickle down my cheek.

Riggs was nearby, turning over rocks, absorbed in his search for treasure or war relics.

"This place does something to you. We should never have come up here," I muttered.

"What?"

"Nothing, man... nothing."

As we all walked out onto the adjacent dirt road, I stopped and turned to have a last look. A light breeze swept across my face. It was a sad place. The old dead trees, scrawny and barren, stood sentinel, mere shadows of their former glory—just like the fort itself.

The old dead trees—the last witnesses to a gruesome massacre.

.

The road up to Signal Mountain

The road up to Signal Mountain was just on the other side of Highway QL-1 and rose abruptly in a slope greater than fifteen degrees. Our pace slowed, and our breathing became labored as we began to tire. We trudged up the steep hill a step at a time, one foot in front of the other. It was slow going. The road turned into a very narrow semi-paved track lined with elephant grass on either side.

I noticed that the group, who had been talking up a storm until now, had become very quiet. We were all getting very nervous. A sudden feeling of absolute stupidity came over me. What in the world were we doing outside the safety of our perimeter? Who in their right mind would go out looking for Viet Cong? And... what if we found them?

I had the eerie, horrible feeling that we were all dead. We were just a bunch of stupid kids waiting to get shot.

"You know, this is a bit spooky," announced Johnny Dees, his voice restrained. "This grass is a perfect hiding place for all kinds of things: Viet Cong, pythons, tigers. Who knows what else!"

We all looked at each other, none willing to dispute the obvious: Dees was correct.

"There was a very large tiger killed down in the bay just over a year ago," said Beckman. "I've never seen a tiger, and I sure would like to keep it that way." He unslung his M-16, chambered a round, and carried it in both hands, ready for action at a moment's notice. In the next instant, everyone had their weapons at the ready. All up and down the line, "click-click-click," a round chambered in each one. We all glanced around at our immediate surroundings, our mood taking an abrupt somber note.

"You know that there are leopards, rhinos, and bears in addition to the tigers," I added.

"Just keep your eyes and ears open," Beckman said.

Tiger killed by South Koreans in Vung Ro Bay

We had come to the conclusion that we had undertaken a ridiculous adventure. The odds of finding bodies from the night before were very slim. The odds of someone finding *our* bodies tomorrow morning became a growing concern. Up to this point, we had been hiking in a tight-knit group, allowing ease of conversation. Beckman decided that we should spread out for our own safety, with Rinslow becoming the point man, then Dees, Riggs, Beckman, and me bringing up the rear. There was no more than fifty feet between each man.

We had been climbing for what seemed like an eternity. My legs were aching. It was hot. I wanted to sit down under a shade tree with a nice, cold beer.

"Lee, do you think we should go back?" I asked, sweat pouring down my forehead.

"Yeah, I second that motion," piped Johnny Dees.

"No," Beckman replied. "By now, the whole base knows we're heading up here. We've got to finish."

What if we get killed in an ambush?" Dees asked.

"Look, the Koreans did a sweep through here yesterday. There are no Viet Cong." Riggs said.

"Can you guarantee that?" Dees was getting worried.

"Well... no."

We were less than a half-mile from the peak of the mountain and the Signal Company stationed there. We were hoping for one of their trucks to come along, but the road remained quiet and unsettling. We were concentrating on any abnormal sound, any movement of the grasses, any strange menacing tiger noises. We were all ready to let loose with a barrage of automatic weapons fire at any moment.

We continued our arduous hike along the rutted old wheel tracks that led up the mountain, too far along now to turn back. We would all have had to admit that we were scared if we turned around now. So, we continued on—up, up, up, towards the top of the mountain.

Bringing up the rear of the formation allowed me a unique opportunity to view the group; my very close friends all stretched out in a line in front of me, hoping not to run into any Viet Cong guerillas hiding in the grass, waiting in ambush. I wondered what we would do. Rinslow, in the lead, would get killed immediately. Most point men usually did. Then it would be up to me, Beckman, Riggs, and Dees to fight off the enemy. A frightening scenario. I was at least thankful that I was with a bunch of battle-tested guys. There were a couple of new MPs in the unit who had just arrived in-country, but neither wanted to go on the mission. Scared, I guess. Or smart. I was happy about that. I knew that the brave men I was with would go down fighting.

Still, the whole thing was a pretty stupid idea. I wanted to turn around and run back down the mountain as fast as I could run.

We came upon a small clearing and decided to take a much-needed break. We opened our canteens and relaxed.

"You know," Riggs said. "I've even heard they have wild boar up here. They're supposed to be pretty mean too. I've never seen one, though."

"I have," I said and told them the story...

•

I was a teenager, 13 or 14, and had attended a Boy Scout Jamboree in the Black Forest near Giessen, Germany. There were well over a thousand scouts from many different countries at the event. We were paired with boys from various nations into large 12-man tents. Many of the scouts spoke no English whatsoever.

Late one night, around 11:00 p.m. or so, one of the German scouts, Hans was his name—I'll never forget that—came up with the brilliant plan to sneak out of camp, cross a small mountain, and visit a Girl Scout camp a couple of miles away.

Ten or eleven of us set out a little after midnight. Several of the boys, who spoke no English at all, just went along because they happened to be in our tent. All they knew was that the rest of us were going somewhere—they didn't know where or why—but they decided to tag along anyway.

I never did understand how I had fallen victim to such an idiotic idea. It was dark. Only one person knew where we were going. We had no water or provisions of any kind. It was cold, and what would we do when we got to the other camp in the middle of the night—wake everybody up?

Nonetheless, we trudged on up the mountain; a damp, cool, foggy smell became stronger and stronger as we ventured further into the forest. A sky full of bright stars provided diffused illumination for our journey. The view, even in darkness, was incredible. I could barely make out the lush green canopy of vast dense forests that stretched for miles. I could hear the gentle rustling of the leaves fighting with the wind. Somewhere, far in the distance, a gentle waterfall cascaded over the edge of a cliff. Frogs were croaking happily. The night air had the magical freshness about it that only October could bring. I sensed a strong pine aroma; the slight breeze had a little bit of a chill to it. It was, all in all, I had decided, an enjoyable nighttime trek.

I smelled them before I heard them.

We had hiked almost a mile and were in the process of climbing a steep incline. My labored breathing suddenly came under attack with the damp, musky odor of what can best be described as someone's 10-day old underarms. It was a smell that almost knocked me over.

Then we heard noises ahead.

"Qu'est-ce que c'est?" asked one. We all stopped and strained to listen.

The noises became louder and louder: a guttural snorting combined with a mean, angry mountain lion groan.

We all stood frozen. None of us had ever heard anything like it before. Whatever it was, it was coming right at us, grunting, groaning, and snorting!

It sounded like a bad horror movie.

The German kid, who had been in the lead, came flying past me, a look of absolute terror on his face. He was going back downhill.

"Wild boars! Run!"

All at once, every one of us turned and ran back down the mountain, as fast, or faster, than our feet would carry us! I ran harder than I'd ever run in my entire life. I ran so quickly that, at times, I feared I might trip over my own feet. I could feel the blood rushing through my heart. I felt like it might explode at any moment. All I could hear behind me was the deep-throated snort of the most vicious animal I'd ever encountered.

It was a horrible, unforgettable sound.

We ran for what seemed like an eternity, the boars closing in on us. I never knew how many there were. It seemed to me like a hundred, although it was probably only three or four.

At the forefront of the group and out of sight, the German kid yelled back to us, "We won't make it. Get up a tree—quick!"

I came upon one boy who had stopped and seemed to be in a state of shock. He spoke no English. He was just looking around at everyone, bewildered. I grabbed his arm, shook him, and pointed up a tree.

We all scrambled up the nearest tree we could find, our hearts struggling to keep a beat.

At first, my feet didn't want to climb the tree that I had chosen. I had reached up as high as I could, grabbed a limb, and tried to scramble up, but both feet just kept sliding back down the tree trunk.

The wild boars were directly behind me, grunting, groaning, and snorting. I couldn't turn my head to look. They might take my leg off. After calming down enough to get both feet to work, I scrambled up the tree, realizing that I would probably end up as dinner if I didn't.

I huddled high up in the branches of an elm tree, halfway down the hillside. I was petrified. My left leg was trembling, out of control, and I had a very difficult time breathing. I attempted to be as quiet as possible, alternating between holding my breath and then gulping down quick shots of air.

Be quiet! Be quiet!

One boy started to cry.

I couldn't see any of the boars, but I could hear them rummaging around, looking for anything—or anyone. All the boys were scattered about the hillside, safe, resting in the trees, and scared to death.

Whimpers and sniffles echoed throughout the forest.

One is afforded plenty of time for reflection while sitting high up in a tree, hiding from wild boars. It didn't take me very long to conclude that this was, without a doubt, the most stupid thing I had ever done. I was more scared than I'd ever been in my entire life—even more scared than the time I rode my bike past old Mrs. Stanford's house. By accident, she had left her front gate open, and, as I rode by, her big black German Shepard came roaring out of the gate, ready to eat me alive.

I just wanted to go home.

After an hour or so, the boars tired of the chase and ambled back up the mountain. We waited for a long, long time before we dared venture from our tree perches. When we did come down, we ran as fast as we could back to camp and the safety of our tent.

That night, while bundled up in my sleeping bag fighting back the tears, I promised myself two things: 1) never to visit Germany again, and 2) that I would never be a party to another stupid adventure.

Now, less than six years later, here I was... right in the middle of another one!

.

"I see it," yelled Dees, oblivious to any imminent danger from hidden Viet Cong. "Off to the left, up on the hill."

We had come around a curve in the road, and the massive sandbagged gated bunker of the signal compound came into view. We still had close to a ¼-mile to trek, but now we somehow felt safe.

"Why don't we all close ranks and march in formation," Beckman said. "No sense in having the bunker guards think we're Viet Cong."

The road leveled out a bit, giving us a chance to catch our breath, then rose up a very steep hill to the bunker and main gate.

As we approached the gate, two bunker guards peered out at us. "Where the hell are you guys from?"

"Down at the bay," answered Beckman. "We just dropped by to see if you guys needed anything."

Signal Mountain – the summit

The bunker guard looked at us like we were stupid and then waved us in.

Several radio communications people came out, welcomed our little group, and offered us a guided tour of the compound. It was situated right on the very top of a mountain peak, strewn with very large boulders. The buildings and roads had been built in and among the boulders. The buildings were all wood frame with a tin roof, and the occupants had placed sandbags in strategic areas across the top. The site was sprinkled with tall scraggly trees, offering not a hint of shade. Large communication dishes of all shapes and sizes filled the rest of the landscape.

"We never get visitors up here," one of the sergeants said. "You guys must have hiked a long way to get up here."

"We did, Sarge," said Beckman. "It was a bit longer of a hike than we expected."

Laughter engulfed the group as the sergeant showed us around the base some more.

"We're pretty safe up here," the sergeant continued. "Sometimes the gooks will lob mortars up here, but we're at the very top of this mountain, so we always have the height advantage."

Signal Mountain – Vung Ro Bay

The view from the top of the mountain was incredible. The western side was nothing but vegetation, mountains, and rocks. In contrast, the eastern side provided broad vistas of the bay, the ocean, and the South Korean White Horse Division compound, situated halfway back down the mountain.

Just beyond the Korean Compound, I could make out the narrow, twisting two-lane Highway QL-1. I looked out over the horizon. "Look how far away the bay is." I motioned to Beckman. "It looks like it's twenty miles from here."

After over an hour of visiting the neighbors, Beckman decided it was time to head back down the mountain. The adventure had already taken the better part of the day.

"Should we ask them for a ride back?" I said. "It's a long hike back down that mountain."

"Hell no," Beckman retorted. "We'd never live that down. These guys come down to the bay all the time to get water. They'd be sure to tell someone sooner or later. No, we hiked up here—we'll hike back down. Just keep your weapons at the ready, just in case."

"Yeah," said Dees. "There's probably a tiger waiting to eat us on the way back."

"You might be right, Johnny," laughed Beckman. "Maybe you better take point."

The Korean Compound and Highway QL-1

Walking back down the dirt road towards the bay

19. July the 4th

One morning I was returning from the shower and heard the wind howling in the distance. I turned and looked up the mountain behind me. The Signal Corps units stationed up on top of the mountain were barely visible. I stood there and watched as the topography disappeared into a fog-like mist, totally obscuring Vung Ro Mountain and even the Korean compound resting at a lower altitude. It was going to be a miserable, dreary, rainy day.

I decided to duck into the dayroom.

There was a group sitting around the bar drinking—what else—Pabst Blue Ribbon. We liked it because the initials were the same as our boats—PBR. Johnny Dees was seated near the door.

"You know, July the 4th is right around the corner. I really miss the fantastic fireworks shows we had back home in Pomeroy, Ohio."

"Yeah, we had great fireworks in Chicago," another added.

"Man, the best ones by far were in New York City," one of the bunker guards threw in. "We used to travel for three hours just to go see those!"

Several of the others began discussing their various back-home fireworks experiences. A few more beers were consumed, and before you knew it, a plan to have the grandest fireworks display in Vung Ro Bay history was hatched! We opened more beers as the excitement grew.

"Someone find a pad and some pencils," Dees said. "We've got to get this all planned out! We need to figure out what we're going to need and who's going to be involved."

"In order for this thing to succeed, it's going to be necessary to involve every bunker on the base," Riggs added. "We're going to need as much bang as possible. We'll need to plan and coordinate everything between the boat crews, bunker guards, and whoever else we can round up."

"Hey, maybe we can get the Koreans to fire off some stuff," said Dees.

"They don't do Fourth of July," Riggs announced.

We determined very early that our NCOIC and the base commanding officer, a Chief Warrant Officer, had to be kept in the dark, or the plan would probably fail.

Hebert and Dees removing red tracer rounds

"I don't think that will be much of a problem," quipped McCall. "I heard the NCOIC tell Beckman that he's going to Qui Nhon for a few days. As for the CO, we'll swear all the bunker guards to secrecy, and by the time he finds out, it will be too late."

Johnny Dees and I volunteered to assemble the .50 caliber belts for the event. It would necessitate removing all the red tracer rounds, every fifth shell, from existing belts, then constructing new belts made of nothing but tracer rounds. A couple of days later, after raiding the ammo Conex several times, we were finished.

There were enough tracer-only belts to supply all three .50 caliber machine guns on both PBRs.

During one of the planning sessions, Riggs decided that not only would the bunker guards be popping parachute flares, but the PBR crewmembers who were not on the boats would go down on the DeLong Pier and fire off red flares to add to the effect. Parachute flares came in handheld aluminum tubes that launched a small rocket for illumination purposes.

July the Fourth arrived with anticipation. The entire base knew of the night's planned activities, and most of the personnel were participating. Word had spread like wildfire. It was going to be the event of the season!

All of the bunkers had stockpiled several cases of white parachute flares, the two PBRs were loaded with red tracer belts for all six .50-caliber machine guns, and two cases of red distress flares had been stacked on the engine hatches.

Several members of the PBRs spent the better part of the afternoon scurrying around the base, making sure that everyone would be in the right place at the right time and do what they had to do, all at the same time. Those not involved in the planning spent the afternoon in the dayroom, trying to whittle down the stock of Pabst Blue Ribbon.

The NCOIC, as anticipated, departed the base the morning of July 3rd. The base CO knew nothing. Everything had gone as planned.

It was 9:00 p.m. on the dot. Everyone on base was either lining the shore or watching the event in the bay from wherever they were. The bunker guards were all facing the bay, oblivious to anything outside the perimeter behind them.

All of a sudden, it sounded like World War III had broken out at Vung Ro Bay! Machine guns started spitting out red lines of fire. Red and white flares were illuminating the night sky from one side of the bay to the other. Tracers from one of the PBRs were streaking skyward in a fan-shaped arch while the other boat fired fore and aft across the mouth of the bay. In addition to flares, the bunker guards had an additional person with them who was firing their machine guns with regular tracer belts. Some of the truck drivers from the 119th Transportation Company were shooting M-79 grenades into the hills... anything to make noise. It was quite a scene! Flares from bunkers were popping off everywhere. The crew on the pier set them off as fast as they could retrieve them from the wooden packing cases. Soldiers were dropping concussion grenades off the side of the pier to add a bit of bang to the event.

The dark, black night sky was ablaze with bullets, flares, more flares, and lots of noise—what a spectacular scene.

It was the Fourth of July!

I wondered what the poor Viet Cong must have been thinking. I hoped none were in the line of fire, or better yet...

July 4th, 1970

20. The Great Outhouse Disaster

The crew of the 458th took great pride in their pink outhouse. It had become something of a local legend among the various units in the bay and visiting soldiers from other locales. Everyone sooner or later would learn of the famous "Pink Outhouse of Vung Ro Bay."

It was a couple of weeks after July 4th. I was walking down the hill from the mess hall, having just finished my lunch. I was on the night shift and had another five hours to go until I went out on patrol. I sauntered along, kicking the red clay dirt clods, not paying mind to much of anything.

The sound of two large rotors commanded my immediate attention. *Whop-whop-whop.* The noise was deafening.

I looked out towards the bay to witness a lumbering Chinook helicopter with fore and aft rotor blades coming in to land at the tiny Vung Ro Heliport.

Chinooks never landed in Vung Ro.

"Hey!" I yelled to Tommy Young, who had been sitting on a wooden bench outside the dayroom chewing on a toothpick. "What do you think's going on with this?"

"No clue. I've never seen one come in here before."

Beckman soon arrived on the scene, awakened from his sleep by the inbound chopper's deafening roar. "What's going on?"

The helicopter was on final approach to the tiny landing pad, typically used only by the much smaller Huey helicopters.

"What are they doing coming in here?" I yelled at Beckman.

"Oh yeah... they had to order some emergency ammo and stuff. We've only got a one-day supply of .50 caliber ammo left for the entire base. They're supposed to bring in a couple of pallets for us. We sure went through an awful lot of stuff on July the 4th. We're about out of everything: ammo, flares, grenades, all of it."

I couldn't help but smile. Beckman knew all the spent shells were headed to Seoul. The Koreans were very happy with us!

Chinook on approach to Vung Ro Helipad

A small crowd soon gathered outside the PBR hootch, all anticipating the arrival of the beast. The chopper came in low over the beach, flying directly over the top of the PBR compound. I looked up and could see the pilot's face. He waved.

The downwash from the rotors was enormous and blew the beach sand about like a dust storm. The PBRs and Boston whaler at the dock were straining at their moorings, first being pulled away from the dock and then shoved back into it.

The huge helicopter flew over the top of the PBR hootch and made a very gentle landing on the helo pad.

A few minutes later, old Papa-San, the 458th handyman, came hobbling around the corner of the dayroom, waving his hands in a frantic state of panic. "Fire—Fire! I no sheet—I no sheet! Numbah ten, Numbah ten!" he yelled, pointing towards the beach and using up most of his English vocabulary. "Fire! Fire!"

"What the hell's he babbling about?" Beckman asked.

"Sounds like he set our sheets on fire!" Young answered.

Beckman, Young, and I sprang into action and ran around the corner of the building, leaving Papa-San standing there pointing and yelling.

"No sheet—No sheet!"

A horrific scene confronted us upon our arrival. Papa-San had been engaged in daily chores, one of which was burning the outhouse waste in a 55-gallon drum cut in half. Papa-San would open a small trap door at the back of the outhouse, slide the half-drum out, pour in a 50/50 mixture of gasoline and diesel fuel, and set fire to it. The odor of this necessary daily ritual was not pleasant. He had been in the middle of this task when the big helicopter came hovering across the beach. The downwash was so powerful that it had knocked the famous Pink Outhouse of Vung Ro Bay over backward, the crumpled structure landing on top of the raging diesel-fueled inferno behind it. It went up like a lit match.

It didn't take long before the entire detachment was on the scene. Some had hand-held fire extinguishers, but the blaze was too much.

The Pink Outhouse on fire!

The Vung Ro Bay Fire Department, a one-truck unit, arrived within a short amount of time. The structure was too far gone to save. The Fire Chief and the three contractor Vietnamese firefighters uncoiled a fire hose down the hill. None of them were probably over a hundred pounds soaking wet. When the three little firefighters got to the outhouse, they all took positions on the hose as the Chief turned the valve at the truck on full blast. The hose lifted the three firefighters off the ground, flung them around, and pounded them into the sand. The Chief cut the water supply, and the crew regained their footing and started over again, this time with less force. The firemen extinguished the inferno a short time later.

Vung Ro Bay Fire Dept. extinguishes the blaze

The pride and joy of the 458th Sea Tigers and Johnny Dee's masterpiece creation was destroyed. The entire crew felt like we had lost a part of our identity. The outhouse was a part of our lives. People knew who we were because of the Pink Outhouse.

As bad as it was to lose our iconic outhouse, there were severe practical implications. Our outhouse was the only one in the entire area. All the others were a good distance away, either further down the beach or up on various hillsides surrounding the bay. Worse yet, there were no restroom facilities on the boats—none at all.

Johnny Dees, Papa-San, and SFC Brown set out to build a new outhouse. Several of us thought that Papa-San felt he was responsible for the event, so we made sure he was heavily involved in the rebuild, which started that afternoon—time was of the essence. Whoever was not out on patrol would scrounge up lumber or steal whatever was necessary to accomplish the task. The lumber yard was just up the hill from the PBR compound and became a quick and easy source. The wood was brought down to the compound and piled up next to the ammo bunker, where SFC Brown would give directions on how long to make each board, then they would be hand-sawed by the crew.

"Sarge," yelled Johnny Dees. "We've got the piece of plywood ready to go on for the seat, but we need a jigsaw to cut a hole out in the middle of it."

"What do you mean?" answered SFC Brown.

"The framing is all ready, and we've got the plywood in place across the top, but we can't put the toilet seat on until we cut a hole in the plywood. We need a jigsaw."

"A jigsaw! Where the hell do you think you are, son? We don't have any jigsaws here," answered the Sarge, quite amused at the situation. Construction ground to a halt. A hand saw was useless to make a round hole with, and that was all that was available.

"Do you think anyone else in the bay might have a jigsaw?" Dees asked.

"I really do doubt it, son," the Sarge answered. "I haven't seen a jigsaw since I left the States."

McCall was standing nearby, intent on watching the progress.

I was on my way from the dock and had stopped for a moment. "Do you think they'll have something ready soon?"

"It's not looking real good. Nobody can figure out how to put a hole in the middle." A smile eased across McCall's face.

"Damn," he exclaimed. "I've got it! Wait right here." He turned and ran off towards the hootch, bounded up the rear steps, and ran into the hallway, heading for his room.

Less than five minutes later, he reappeared with his .45 caliber pistol in his hand and three extra clips of ammunition. "OK, everyone, step back!"

He went over to the construction site, picked up the toilet seat, and laid it in place. Then he traced an outline of the desired hole with a pencil, removed the piece of plywood off the framework, and placed it on its end. He made the outline a little heavier with the pencil, stepped back, cocked the pistol, and fired one shot—right on the line. Then another, and another, and another—all the way around the circle. He had to change magazines twice, but finally, there was enough of a hole in the plywood that he could easily chisel out the remainder with a screwdriver and a hammer.

Proud of his expertise, McCall picked up the toilet seat and laid it in its new resting place. The crew broke out into enthusiastic and appreciative applause.

Unfortunately, Papa-San took sick for almost a week, and construction on the outhouse came to a screeching halt. We could have quickly finished it without him, but we all knew he regarded it as 'his baby,' and for anyone to interfere in the completion would have hurt his feelings. All that we had in place was the framework and a toilet seat. For the next several days everybody waited until it got dark to use the outhouse.

Nobody wanted to be a sniper's target.

Papa-San eventually painted the new outhouse O.D. green. None of us wanted a pink one—it just wouldn't have been the same.

The new seat in place – complete with a hole in it!

21. Foolish Escapades

Young men in their late teens think they're invincible. The crew at Vung Ro was no different. Lee Beckman had a friend of his come down from Qui Nhon one day for a visit. They hadn't seen each other in several months. Beckman was on the night shift that week and decided to let his friend accompany them on patrol that night so they could talk and socialize. His friend had never been on a PBR. Then, just before crew call, Beckman announced to the rest of the crew that they could all have the night off. He and his friend would take the patrol. There were no complaints whatsoever.

Riggs had a good card game going on in the dayroom.

Things had been very quiet in the bay for more than a week. The night shift had been doing what they always did: running out to one of the mooring buoys after dark, tying up, and going to sleep for the night. They would always leave one man on guard duty and rotated the watch every two hours. That was Beckman's plan for the night, even though it meant they would have a more frequent watch cycle with only two men instead of four.

Beckman and his friend, Doug, got aboard the PBR, fired up the big twin diesels, cast off the lines, and set out for a 12-hour patrol. Beckman steered the boat out towards the other side of the bay, running her up to full speed in quick order.

The following day, I came upon Beckman seated in the corner of the dayroom, chugging down beer after beer. He was the only one in there.

"Wow, Lee, What's up, man? You look upset. How did the patrol go last night?"

"Oh, you have no idea."

Then he proceeded to tell me of his adventure on patrol:

"After we got underway, we motored around the bay for a bit, making a quick sweep of the beaches in the various coves, and then we went out into the South China Sea for a mile or so. There was a two to three-foot swell, and the boat was zipping across the waves. When we got to the sea buoy, I turned around and headed back into the bay. We were both having a great time out on the water."

He stopped and took a long chug of Olympia.

"Anyway, it soon began to get dark. I found a spot over by the far side of the bay near Golf Point and dropped anchor. My friend and I spent the next couple of hours talking about all kinds of things: diesel engine repair, girls back home, what we were going to do when we got back to the world, and all. The night quickly turned black—I mean pitch black. With the low cloud cover, there was no moonlight at all and not a star in sight. The wind had died, and the night was very still. Visibility was close to zero. I knew the sea was out there somewhere, but the conditions made it impossible to distinguish the water from the sky. It all blended into one solid mass. It was 360° darkness—as black as black could ever be."

"Oh man," I said. "This is starting to sound like a Riggs story."

"Well, I haven't gotten to the scary part yet."

I smiled and went to get a beer for myself. I felt like I was going to need one, even though it was early morning.

"I started feeling uneasy out there in the quiet still of the night, out on a darkened boat with only me and my friend. The night was doing strange things to me, man. Sometimes, if I looked hard enough, my eyes would play tricks on me. I kept hearing noises in the dark, real quiet noises that scared me half to death. Anyway, I sat on the bow, looking out into the darkness, searching for any foreign shape or sound. The water was flat calm, and smooth as silk. It was very quiet... way too quiet. I had to shake my head a few times to clear my vision. I grabbed a nearby canteen, twisted open the cap, and doused my face with water. My friend, Doug, asked if I was OK. I told him I kept hearing things out in the darkness."

"Are you *sure* you didn't get this from Riggs?" I asked.

"No, no, let me finish. The best part is coming."

"OK, sorry."

"So, we continued whispering on the bow; the waves were calm and gentle, lapping at the hull and making strange noises of their own. I looked at my watch one time, and it was almost midnight. Then out of nowhere, I heard the soft "chug-chug-chug" of a small boat moving through the water. I knew that the darkness and the dark green color of our PBR probably made us invisible, so I motioned for Doug to be quiet. We were still sitting on the bow, just behind the gun tub."

"Maybe I should go get Riggs," I laughed.

"Will you shut up a second!"

"OK, OK."

"Well, out of the darkness comes this sampan, its little engine purring along like a Singer sewing machine. It had no running lights. I thought that it was heading straight for us. I strained to see it in the darkness, trying to get my eyes to focus in the blackness. The little engine's chugging became louder and louder as it passed just yards off our bow. They never even noticed us anchored off to their port side. So, I stood up, leaned over the gun tub, pointed the .50 caliber machine guns in the air, and fired three of four rounds over their heads. The Vietnamese stopped their sampan as fast as possible, turned off their engine, and turned on their running light. Then I hauled up the anchor and started the engines. I motored over to the sampan and pulled up alongside. Doug grabbed a line from one of the fishermen and secured it to the port midships cleat on the PBR. I shut the engines down so I could hear better and communicate with Doug if I needed to."

"Wow, Lee, you really disregarded well-established standard operating procedure—and common sense," I laughed.

"Yeah, well, as you'll soon learn, sometimes I do really stupid stuff."

"OK, so what happened next?"

"I handed Doug an M-16, told him to cover me, and I jumped down into the sampan to search for contraband."

"You what!" I exclaimed.

"Yeah, yeah, I know. I regretted my impulsiveness the instant I landed on the deck. The dim glow from the single running light on the sampan let me see that we were outnumbered. There were six Vietnamese on board. I wondered what I would do if they decided to attack. I was worried about Doug's ability to provide security over the situation. I was unsure of his battlefield skills. I know what to expect from the MPs, you know? I wondered what would happen if Doug got scared and surrendered. I regretted not bringing the coxswain and two MPs along. Anyway, several thoughts raced through my mind—none of them pretty. I thought of my family back home. What would my mother think when she discovered that I had died performing such an irrational and reckless venture?"

"Oh man, you're pretty upset, aren't you?'

"Yeah, it's the dumbest thing I've ever done. I could just see the officer in my mother's living room telling her that I would have still been alive had I not jumped into a sampan full of Viet Cong in the middle of the pitch-black night with only one man as a back-up."

"Yeah, that would've been sad," I added.

"Well, it didn't take me long to realize what a foolish undertaking it was. I completed a very quick cursory inspection of the vessel and scrambled back aboard the PBR, thankful that nothing had gone awry. I didn't bother to check under any of the floorboards. I didn't want to find any weapons, nor did I want these six fishermen to be Viet Cong. I untied the sampan, gave them a small wave, and started the engines."

"Wow," I said. "Even my nerves are starting to get frazzled."

"Yeah, well, you shoulda been with me. My nerves were so frazzled I decided to cut my shift short by a couple of hours. Neither of us said much on the way back to the dock. Both of us realized how foolish and trusting we had been—how close to death we could have been. So much could have gone wrong. Suppose the Vietnamese had opened up with small arms fire? Worse yet, suppose they had let loose with an RPG, or what if they had overpowered me while I was aboard the sampan? Suppose they had commandeered the PBR?"

"I'll bet you'll never do anything like that again."

"Amen, brother. Amen."

•

The following day Beckman and I were attempting to get to our boat for a regular patrol shift. It was an overcast day with a stiff breeze blowing in from the east. Easterly winds always created problems since the entrance to the bay opened to the east. The waves were crashing in on the dock, making any attempt at getting across the narrow ramp very difficult.

"Where are the MPs?" Beckman inquired, hoping that he wouldn't have to wait too long for them to show up. The PBR rocked at the dock, straining at its moorings, and Beckman wanted to get underway as soon as possible. We could head over to the other side of the bay and find a lee from the wind and waves.

"Whoa, we gotta go through that?" The MPs had shown up, just a couple of minutes late. Beckman, the ranking enlisted man on the boat, said nothing.

It wasn't all that big of a deal.

Waves crashing onto PBR gangway

"OK, guys, you know how this works. Wait for a slight lull in the wave action, and then run for it. If you're lucky enough, you won't get too wet," I said.

Beckman was first, catching just the right moment and dashing through the spray and onto the gangway. He turned and motioned for one of the others to venture across behind him. Just as one of the MPs started across, an unexpected explosion occurred just down the beach. It was followed in rapid succession by several others, all progressing closer and closer. One splashed down at the far end of the floating pier, just beyond the PBR. Beckman had just stepped onto the dock, and everyone else was in the process of coming over. There were two MPs on the gangway, and I had just run through the drenching sea spray. Beckman swung around to ascertain the situation. The Viet Cong were 'walking' mortar rounds in on us—in the middle of the morning.

"Hurry up," he yelled. "We gotta get the hell out of here!"

I scrambled to the coxswain's flat and fired up the engines. "Let the lines go," I yelled to the MPs.

Easing the boat away from the dock, I gradually increased speed until we were safely away from the enemy fire.

"Why are they attacking us in daylight? It's not Friday night."

"We've got that new Army ship, the *John U.D. Page,* arriving in a couple of hours. Maybe they're trying to scare it off. It's supposed to be loaded to the gills with bombs and ammo," said Beckman. "We've got to escort it into the harbor."

We ran the boat across the harbor and ventured out about a mile into the South China Sea, just far enough to get a glimpse of any vessel coming down from the north. The *Page* was in-bound from Qui Nhon, less than one hundred miles to the north.

I brought the throttles back to idle, and we drifted in the calm seas.

"I don't see them yet."

"Let's go back in the bay and tie up to a buoy for a bit," said Beckman. 'They'll be along pretty soon."

PBR escorting Lt. Col John U.D. Page into harbor

US Army vessel Lt. Col John U.D. Page

22. Super Typhoon Kate

Kate formed as a tropical disturbance off the Marshall Islands, tracked westward, and became a typhoon, devastating the island of Mindanao in the Philippines on October 18, 1970. More than 450 people died from high winds and flooding. A strong ridge to its north forced it westward, and it eventually reached Category 4 Super Typhoon strength on October 25 with winds of 155 mph and seas cresting to 25 feet.

It was bearing down on Vung Ro Bay.

It was a Sunday morning. I walked into the radio room just as Beckman was getting off the phone.

"That was the NCOIC," he said. "He's going to be in Qui Nhon for several more days, and he's very concerned about us weathering the typhoon heading our way."

"How bad is it going to be?" I asked.

"I'm not sure what's coming, Three-two. It looks like the damn thing is here already. I've never seen anything like this before," he added.

The rain started, and then the wind picked up. Beckman glanced over at me and then carefully opened the back door, making sure not to let a gust of wind rip it from his hands. He stared at the oncoming storm. He looked up at the ugly black sky forming across the bay. It was headed right towards the base; the entire horizon to the east was a mass of black gloom. He looked out towards the beach and the dock.

The decrepit old dock was bouncing around and taking a beating from the strong winds and high waves. Both PBRs were slamming against the side of the dock in unison with the waves. The mooring lines looked as though they might snap at any moment.

He held his hands over his eyes to shield them from the rain, but the visibility was terrible and getting worse with every passing moment. The storm was gathering strength very rapidly. The wind and rain were beginning to intensify with a vengeance.

Just then, Johnny Dees came running in, soaking wet from head to toe. "Damn, Lee, this looks terrible! What's the plan?"

"This is not looking very good, Johnny." Beckman answered, "The NCOIC is not coming back for a while, so we're on our own. Go and round up a few of the other guys. We're going to have to get these boats out of here, or they'll sink at the dock. Where are the Boston Whalers?"

"They were both moved up onto the beach earlier this morning," replied Dees. "Hebert and a couple of others pulled them out with the truck."

"Yeah, we tried to secure everything we could," I said. "This is a hell of a time for the NCOIC to be gone."

"We've got to abandon our dock," Beckman decided. "This storm is going to rip that old piece of shit to pieces at any minute. We need to get these boats underway immediately and tie them up to the DeLong Pier. We'll have to moor up alongside the LCM boat over there. They're on the north side. All this wind is coming out of the southeast, so we might be okay there."

John Forrest, a new coxswain from Philadelphia, arrived a short time later with two MPs in tow. We had several new people working with us. McCall, Young, and Rinslow had served their time and rotated back stateside several weeks before. Riggs re-enlisted and was sent to Germany.

"We've got to get the boats moved, right now!"

"Looks like I'm all you've got," Forrest said to Beckman.

"O.K. Follow me," Beckman barked and opened the back door again. We fought our way through the biting wind and rain down to the dock. The waves were several feet high and had already managed to destroy most of the gangway across to the pier. All that remained was the single telephone pole used as a support member.

"Are you kidding me!" one of the MPs cried out. "There's no way we can get across that damn pole."

"We've got no choice," said Beckman. "These boats have to be moved—and it has to be *now*! Think of it like a tightrope. Here, I'll go first." He slowly ventured out onto the telephone pole, fighting against the wind and driving rain.

Beckman made it out ten or twelve feet across the pole, one foot in front of the other, arms out for balance. Hitting a slippery spot and almost falling off, he wobbled back and forth but recovered with skill as the wind and rain did their best to blow him into the water. Carefully negotiating his way across the rest of the pole, he managed to get onto the dock without injury.

"See," he yelled back. "Nothing to it! Be careful, though. This dock is slippery as hell."

The rest of us followed with care and caution.

The wind was steady and increasing.

Just then, the regular coxswain for *Captain America* came running down to the dock. He had only been there for a couple of months—a replacement for McCall, who had completed his tour and went home. "Got here as fast as I could, Lee. I was up at the medic shack. A piece of flying lumber whacked me on the head."

"Are you OK?" yelled Beckman.

"Yeah, yeah, I'm fine."

"We've got to hurry," shouted Beckman, his voice faint against the roaring of the wind. "You and the MPs take the *Captain America*. Hebert—you, me, and Forrest will take the other boat."

"Damn, I hate that replacement boat, Lee," I said. "You had mine running like a new one."

"Too bad, three-two, but it's better than nothing."

"Yeah, I suppose so, but I sure as hell don't trust it. It's going to break down any day now."

"Well, we don't have much choice in the matter. It's the only boat they could spare."

"Yeah, because nobody in Qui Nhon wanted it!"

Beckman laughed. "OK, let's go!"

We jumped aboard our respective boats, timing leaps to coincide with the vessels' rise and fall, massive waves running alongside the dock. One of the stern lines on my boat strained suddenly, stretched beyond its breaking limit, and snapped. It sounded like a bullet.

"Hurry! Hurry!" yelled Beckman. "Get those lines untied!" he cried. I already had the engines running and ran around to the starboard midships to let the spring line go just as Forrest released the bow line. Beckman untied the stern line and threw it on the dock. The boat lifted on a wave and swept back towards the beach, stern first.

"Get back to the wheel," screamed Beckman frantically from the stern deck. "Get this boat outta here!"

The next couple of waves would set the boat stern-first onto the beach, destroying the jet drive propulsion units.

I hurried back into the coxswain's flat, swung the wheel hard to port, and threw both throttles full ahead, praying that the starboard stern wouldn't collide with the dock. At that moment, I missed not having the *Magic Christian*. Over the previous several months, Beckman had made all the adjustments necessary to ensure that that boat performed flawlessly. It probably handled and ran better than a new one. The replacement boat sent down from Qui Nhon was a piece of crap, having been run hard with very little maintenance.

"Hurry," yelled Beckman. "Go-Go-Go!"

The boat sprang to life and roared away from the dock, waves crashing over the bow, sea spray cascading over the fragile tubular aluminum canopy supports. I felt the wind rushing through and feared the canvas canopy might rip away. I guided the boat into the waves, and when I thought that I was far enough away from the PBR pier, I brought the throttle controls back a bit, allowing the craft to ride on a more even keel in the raging seas. I looked around and saw *Captain America* not fifty feet from my stern. Beckman was squatting down next to me, behind the dash, trying to keep out of the spray so he could pop his head up occasionally and see what was in front of him.

We arrived at the DeLong pier and managed to tie up, bow facing into the seas, alongside the seventy-eight-foot landing craft assigned to Vung Ro. It was from the 1099th Transportation Company and operated by a crew of five enlisted men and one warrant officer, who was the port Harbormaster and also base Commanding Officer. The enlisted men lived in a hootch they had built on the cargo deck. The warrant officer had an office and a room in one of the barracks buildings on shore.

The three boats rode rather well on the north side of the DeLong Pier, the *Captain America* secured to the landing craft, and my replacement boat tied to the outboard side. Beckman, the coxswain of the *Captain America,* and the MPs got off and took shelter in the hootch on the LCM. Forrest and I remained aboard our boat in case of an emergency.

DeLong Pier

Wind and rain continued to increase the rest of the day in a maelstrom, the likes of which I had never witnessed. The rain was so heavy that *Captain America* started taking on excess water.

"Where's it coming from?" I asked.

"I don't know, and it's raining too hard to go look," Forrest replied. "I'll go get the coxswain. He'll just have to start the engines every couple of hours to operate the bilge pumps."

By mid-afternoon, the coxswain yelled over to me that the bilge pump was not keeping up with the water. He lifted the engine room hatch and saw that water was halfway up the diesel engines. I ran across to the LCM and hollered for Beckman. "I think *Captain America* might sink. If it does, it'll take the other boat down with it."

Everyone ran topside, oblivious to the driving rain and howling wind. Beckman jumped off the side of the LCM and onto the stern deck of *Captain America*. The coxswain opened the hatch again. Water was rising fast. Another few inches and it would be high enough to enter the air intakes, then the engines would shut down, more water would enter, and it would sink. "The only thing we can do is pop the Jacuzzis." Beckman bellowed. "Forrest, hook up the inductor tube!"

The Jacuzzi jet drive pumps drew water in from under the boat, compressed it, and shot it out under enormous pressure through the stern nozzle. The thrust propelled the craft forward. On top of each pump was an inspection plate that one could remove to facilitate debris removal. In an emergency, an adapter plate with a length of flexible hose could be attached, allowing the jet drive to, in essence, be used as a high-speed bilge pump.

Forrest hurried to the forward compartment, returning within moments with the hose and adapter plate. Beckman jumped down into the lazarette, the aft compartment housing the jet drive units, and hastily hooked up the system.

"Fire the engine back up!" He climbed back out of the hold as the engine started shooting the water out.

The pump-out lasted several minutes.

"That seems to have it under control. The water's back to a manageable level," yelled Forrest as he pulled the inductor tube up and replaced the inspection cap. He shut the hatch and shouted to the coxswain to shut the engines down.

Towards evening the winds began to shift around to the north as the storm slowly passed over. Waves along the pier were increasing, so we all took shelter on board the LCM.

The warrant officer on the LCM was becoming very concerned. "We're all going to have to move to the south side of the pier. This is just going to get worse and worse the longer we stay here. We'll need you to get the PBRs underway, then lay off for a little while we make our way around to the other side of the pier. Then you can come alongside and tie up again."

Forrest and I made our way back to our boat, followed by the coxswain and the MPs on the *Captain America*.

The weather was getting progressively worse. The wind was getting stronger, and the rain was coming down harder. Beckman had decided to go up on the DeLong Pier to supervise. He did not appear to be at all comfortable with the situation.

"OK, let's get these boats moved around."

"I think we need to get some life jackets on, don't you?" Forrest asked Beckman.

"Yeah, that's probably not such a bad idea."

We scrounged around the two PBRs and were able to come up with only five life jackets. We needed six. Everyone put one on except Beckman.

"I'll be up on the pier, anyway."

Beckman waved his arms—the pre-arranged signal to go ahead with the movement. Putting the PBR in gear, I took up slack on the spring line. Forrest ran to the stern and cast off, then rushed to the bow, slipping and sliding on the wet decks. He released the line, and I put the boat in neutral for just an instant. Then he let the spring line go, and I put the boat in gear again and added a little throttle. Nothing happened. I added a bit more and more. The boat finally started moving, making a lot of noise, and riding up and down on the waves.

As soon as the vessel was free of the dock, I pushed the throttles further and further down, the engines screaming. The boat started to move.

"It's not doing much, but at least we're moving," I said.

Progress was slow but sure.

The other coxswain followed in the *Captain America*, and soon both of us were riding the waves waiting for the LCM to move. It also had a lot of trouble maneuvering against the high winds and seas. The heavy steel landing craft backed away from the pier and made a quick approach to the structure's south side, managing to get bow, spring, and stern lines over. They were taking a beating. With massive waves rolling down the side of the pier, the sea conditions weren't all that much better on the south side.

I managed to maneuver my PBR alongside the LCM and tied up as best I could. The boat was not sitting well. I scrambled across the stern deck of the LCM and crawled up one of the monstrous tires hanging alongside the pier. I ran over to Beckman. He knew that there was no way the little thirty-two-foot fiberglass PBRs would survive the night tied up where they were.

"How high do you think the waves are?" I asked Beckman. He watched as they rolled in and down alongside the pier.

"I'm not real sure. I'd say six to eight feet. We can't stay here. Those boats are fiberglass and aluminum. They'll get ripped to pieces before morning."

Just about that time, one of the MP's who had volunteered to help out on the *Captain America* climbed up onto the pier.

"This is bullshit. I'm outta here!" he stated curtly and started walking back to the barracks and shelter from the storm. He was still wearing his life jacket.

"What the hell?" Beckman was visibly upset but had no authority over the MP.

"Why don't you just order him back here?" I suggested.

"Sounds good, but I really can't," Beckman answered. "He's MP, and we're attached to the MP's. They run the show here. I'm Transportation. I have no authority over him."

The wind was howling with a fury I had not been exposed to before. I had never seen so much rain.

"I guess we're right in the thick of this damn typhoon," I said. "This wind is easily over a hundred miles an hour."

"We're not going to be able to do this, Three-two," Beckman said.

"What are we going to do? We can't go back to our dock—it's probably not even there. We can't tie up here. There's nowhere else to go. And we don't have enough fuel to sit out here and ride it out all night."

Just then, Forrest came up to us. "This is not looking good. Why don't we try to get to the sheltered water over in the cove? Maybe we can drop anchor there."

"Yeah, that's probably a pretty good idea, John... if we can get over there," replied Beckman.

Beckman, Forrest, and I crawled down a huge tire and dropped onto the LCM deck. Beckman informed the warrant officer of our plans, told the other coxswain to follow us, and we set out across the merciless bay. Waves and wind-driven spray crashed over the boats rendering visibility to near-zero.

We hadn't made more than a half-mile of progress when Beckman shouted, "Let's try to find one of the ships mooring buoys and see if we can tie up to it."

I radioed the other boat with the change of plans. It was now getting dark; visibility was very poor, the wind and rain relentless in their fury. Forrest was under the shelter of the canopy and shining his flashlight back and forth across the water, looking for the mooring buoy. He got up on the engine room hatch and attempted to fire parachute flares to light the area and locate the buoys, but the rain was so intense that the flares would only go up fifteen to twenty feet in the air before plunging into the sea. After firing off a half-dozen flares, he realized it was a futile attempt.

After wandering about the bay, rolling up and down, we finally came across one of the mooring buoys. I couldn't believe how difficult it had been to find. We came out to the buoys all the time, perhaps daily, yet the extreme adverse wind and sea conditions combined with the encroaching darkness made the roiling waters of the bay very unfamiliar indeed.

The buoy was all steel, circular with a wooden rub rail, about eight feet in diameter, and sat four feet above the water. The waves weren't quite as bad as they had been over at the pier.

"I think we might be able to tie up to that," Beckman called from the bow. The boat was bouncing up and down. "Too bad that damn MP took that life jacket. It was the last one we had."

"Here, take mine," I offered. "I'll be OK here in the coxswain's flat."

I eased the boat to the buoy as gently as possible, making sure not to crash into the buoy and destroy the bow. Beckman donned the life jacket and steadied himself on the bow as best he could, holding onto the .50 caliber machine gun barrel for balance. Then, at just the right moment, he jumped down onto the buoy with a bow line in his hand. Forrest stood on the bow hanging onto the forward gun tub. The bow started to rise on the next wave.

"Back off—Back off!" Beckman yelled. "I'm afraid that bow is going to come back down and knock me off this buoy."

I pulled the throttles into reverse. The motion of the boat riding down into a trough at the same time magnified the effect.

"Damn, don't pull me into the water!" he yelled.

I was happy that Beckman had a life jacket. Luck was with us, though, and the bow of the boat rose back up again, just in time. He quickly secured the line to the giant metal ring in the center of the buoy.

"Tying that line to the buoy was the easy part," Beckman said. "Now I've got to get back onto the boat."

The PBR was bobbing violently up and down. I inched up to the buoy, keeping the boat in place as long as I could.

"Stop! Stop!" yelled Forrest.

Struggling against the power of the wind and waves, Beckman knew the timing of his jump had to be perfect. The bow rose high above his head, seemed to hover in midair for a moment, then came crashing back down. Beckman took a flying leap at just the right moment, landing with both feet flat on the gunwale. Forrest tried to grab him but missed. Little did he anticipate that the deck would be slippery from all the water washing over it. Both feet shot out from under Beckman, and he landed in a sitting position on the narrow gunwale surrounding the decks. For an instant, I had a fleeting vision of him flying backward into the sea, but then Forrest reached out at the last minute and grabbed him with one hand, the other clinging to the barrel of the .50-caliber machine gun.

Beckman jumped up smiling, holding on for his life, and inched his way back to the coxswain's flat.

"Wow! Let's not do that again. When we leave here, we'll just cut the damn line. I could have been killed out there!" Beckman's voice was sharp with irritation. "And that damn MP took that life jacket with him when he went back to the barracks. We really needed that!"

Forrest inched his way back to the coxswain's flat. "Wow! That was a close call. I thought you were a goner, Lee."

The other PBR approached behind us. Beckman threw them a line and secured our end to the stern cleat. They caught it on the first attempt and made it fast to their bow cleat. Then the two boats shut down the engines, confident in knowing we were as safe as we could be, riding out the storm and facing into the raging gale and roiling sea.

I hailed the other coxswain on the radio. "PBR 29, are you guys OK?"

"Yep," came the reply. "We're wet, cold, hungry, sad, and lonely. Other than that, we're fine."

Both crews retreated to the cramped confines of the below-decks radio room. We had two large thermos jugs of water and enough C-Rations to last a week—another of the new NCOIC's directives. He had both boats stocked with a week's worth of provisions.

"Just in case," he had told us. In the past, the crews would simply grab whatever they needed for the day out of the storage Conex up on the beach.

I ventured up on deck several times during the storm to check the lines. They were as taut as they could ever be. I remembered from my boat training that nylon lines have a 60% stretch factor. I was nervous all night, certain the line tied to the mooring buoy would snap at any moment, and we would all crash upon the jagged rocks of the bay before the light of day. I started back down below deck, stopped, and glanced off towards the beach. It was so dark all I could see was the white water crashing on the shore—wave after wave after wave of relentless white surf.

Sleep was impossible; the boats were rolling and rocking in the heaving seas all night long. I wondered how the guys on shore were doing as the typhoon was sure to inflict severe damage to the base.

Hell, I thought, was there even any base left?

Both boats rode out the worst of the typhoon tied to the mooring buoy. There appeared to be a lull by early morning, with the waves having calmed down quite a bit inside the bay. The *Captain America* untied their line and rode over to the DeLong Pier to let the LCM crew know that no one had perished at sea during the night.

The base had sustained severe damage from the typhoon. The pier at the PBR base was gone. The only thing left was a few pilings.

"We need to get ashore and see what's left," said Beckman.

"How are we going to do that?" I asked. "There's nowhere to tie up."

"We'll just have to swim in," announced Beckman.

"PBR 29," I called over the radio. "Follow us. We're going to the shallows off Charlie Beach to anchor. We're going ashore."

"Roger that. Right behind you," came the reply.

We motored the two PBRs over to a small beach near the base and anchored. Then we waded ashore, leaving one person aboard each boat to help us get back aboard. We all went ashore with .45 caliber pistols drawn, just in case, holding them high overhead to keep them dry.

I followed Beckman, Forrest, and an MP down a narrow spit of beach and rounded a rocky point just north of the concrete ramp used for the LST ships and LCUs. The three of them had nothing to say when they came upon the destruction. The once pristine white sandy beach was littered with debris, pieces of wooden buildings, and tree limbs. One of the two Boston Whaler boats that had been hauled high up the beach earlier was missing, and the other was upside down near the water's edge. Most of the buildings were gone or severely damaged. The maintenance shack, located on the concrete slab behind the Quonset hut, was now resting on the beach, broken into pieces. Much to everyone's surprise, the Quonset hut was in fair condition, with minor damage to the roof and both doors. There were a few big dents in the sides from flying debris.

"Wow!" exclaimed Forrest. "This is incredible."

"Yeah, we'd better see how the rest of the guys are doing. It's awfully quiet around here," said Beckman.

We all stopped for a moment, realizing how deserted everything was after Beckman's words. There wasn't a single sign of activity anywhere. We made our way up the beach past the ammo Conex and rounded the corner of our dayroom. The storm had blown the roof off, and furniture inside was scattered about, but the refrigerator was there, and the bar was still intact.

Forrest pushed the screen door out of the way and stepped inside.

"Check for beer!" I yelled.

He crawled over a few upside-down tables and chairs, reached the refrigerator, and opened the door.

"Bingo!" he yelled. "It's half full. Here. I'll pass some to you."

We all sat down on the stoop outside the dayroom and enjoyed our little bit of luxury. It felt like we were in a no man's land or something.

Where was everybody?

"OK, let's get going," Beckman said, downing the last sip of his Olympia.

We got up and walked around to the front of the PBR compound, looking for anyone at all.

The rickety old mess hall that used to be up on the hill across the road was nowhere in sight.

"Hey!" came a shout from down the road, in the direction of the stevedore barracks area.

We looked over that way as a group of 30 or 40 men headed towards us.

"Are you guys all that's left?" yelled Beckman.

"Oh, hell no!" one answered. "We're all OK. Nobody's dead. Everybody else is holed up in the barracks back there."

In conversing with them, we found out that the other soldiers stationed on the base had taken shelter under the perimeter bunkers or in a few more substantial buildings, such as the barracks. There had been no fatalities or severe injuries. Most of the buildings, however, were gone.

We returned to the beach, righted the overturned Boston Whaler, set it in the water, and pulled it back to the anchored PBR's.

"How about you guys take that Whaler in tow?" Beckman asked the other coxswain.

•

We returned to the LCM, which was still tied up to the DeLong pier. We managed to tie up alongside with the assistance of several tires that had been found scattered around the pier. They helped to keep the boats from smashing into each other so much.

The LCM had a more powerful radio than we did, and after consulting with headquarters at Qui Nhon, we were ordered to abandon Vung Ro Bay.

"I'll be damned!" said Beckman. "The NCOIC wants us to send a coxswain up to Qui Nhon with the convoy. They're short-handed up there. I guess we'll send the *Captain America* coxswain."

"That's crazy," I said. "We need all the help we can get."

"Nothing we can do. Orders. I'll take PBR 29. You and Forrest run the other one."

We all boarded our respective boats again, and motored back over to the shallow water near Charlie Beach. We dropped our anchors and waded ashore.

The 454th Transportation Company had several trucks that were already on the base. We loaded them in haste with whatever we could salvage quickly. Stevedores from the 854th Transportation Company ran and jumped onto their front-end loaders and piled ammunition and bombs onto the beds of several tractor-trailers. Nothing was organized. *Just get it and go!* was the order of the day. Whatever couldn't be loaded on the trucks would be destroyed.

Nothing could fall into enemy hands.

Fat Cook, the Kentucky knife thrower, and several others all piled into the back of a deuce and a half that had been loaded with foodstuffs and supplies for the journey up Highway QL-1 to Qui Nhon.

Meanwhile, the PBR contingent was trying to organize things at our compound. Allocated a small space on one truck, in addition to our three-quarter-ton, we had to pick and choose what we wanted to ship to Qui Nhon, what had to go on the boats, and what would be destroyed or left behind.

Luckily, my room hadn't been destroyed. The roof was severely dented and cracked open, but all of my belongings were intact. I opened my locker door.

"Well, glad to see you made it through all that," I said to the Mystery Girl.

I had just walked out of the remnants of the dayroom when one of the bunker guards came rushing up to me with $30 in his hand. "Hebert, this is all I've got! I really want your stereo. You can't take it on the boat with you. It'll get ruined."

He had been pestering me about it for months, to no avail. I reached out and took the money. "It's in my room. Help yourself. Be careful of the door. It's not in the best of shape anymore."

The other coxswain, two boat engineers, and the rest of the MP's all piled into our three-quarter truck and waved goodbye as they positioned themselves in the convoy line.

The convoy of eleven trucks set out with darkness approaching. They had no choice. They had to go. The base Commanding Officer had placed a call to Tuy Hoa earlier requesting a gun truck escort.

It never arrived.

Fat Cook and the rest had their weapons at the ready, waiting for anything. All of the trucks were on full alert, weapons loaded, no one at rest.

I watched the convoy of trucks pull out of the compound, one by one. At that moment, I was so thankful that truck driving school had been full back when I was in basic training.

What had I been thinking?

We were about to return to the PBRs when one of our puppies came scampering from behind the maintenance shed on the beach. Soon, the rest appeared and started barking excitedly at us, happy to see familiar faces.

"Lee, what about the dogs?" Forrest asked Beckman. Nobody had thought about the dogs.

"The trucks have already gone. What are we going to do? The gooks will eat them if we leave them here. And there's no way we can take them on the boats with us."

Beckman stopped and stared at the dogs on the beach, lost in thought. We all looked at each other; we knew the answer, but nobody wanted to say it. After a few moments, Beckman whispered to the MP.

"You two come with me, back to the boats."

We walked down to the water's edge and made our way around the rocky outcropping, losing sight of the bay and the devastation. We were in the middle of climbing back aboard the boats when we heard seven gunshots echo in the distance.

23 The Evacuation

We returned to the relative safety of mooring alongside the landing craft.

"What are we going to do now?" I asked Beckman. "We don't have a base left. Everybody's gone."

"Well, we're going up to Qui Nhon by sea," replied the warrant officer on board the LCM. "It's eighty-four nautical miles from here, so normally a ten to twelve-hour run at eight knots. I don't think we'll be making *that* kind of speed, though," he added, grinning. "We've got plenty of fuel for all three boats. We've got plenty of C-rations. We've got enough ammo. There's nothing else we *can* do."

We made preparations as best we could, running a hose from the LCM to top off the fuel tanks on both PBRs. We tied down everything we could think of, knowing that the sea, still angry from the typhoon, would pose a significant problem.

Onshore, things were different as we went about preparing; our dispirited crew spent the afternoon watching the base—their former home—being ransacked by local Vietnamese and ARVN soldiers. I don't know how they found out so quickly about us leaving. They tore apart whatever they could, hauling the loot away in trucks, carts, or lashed to the sides of bicycles.

We spent our last night tied off to the sea buoy again, hoping we wouldn't be attacked. The camp was deserted, and while our radio could reach the Koreans up on the mountain, we knew that, in the event of an attack, getting any help from them was unlikely.

We had nothing to trade.

The typhoon had passed, but the ocean was still stirred up. It would take several days for it to calm down, and that meant misery for everyone aboard.

The three boats set off at daybreak the next morning. The LCM, with the warrant officer in charge, was the lead boat, followed by the *Captain America* with Beckman at the helm, along with an MP, and then my boat bringing up the rear, with Forrest on board. Beckman had decided to run *Captain America* himself. He was towing the surviving Boston Whaler.

LCM departing Vung Ro Bay

"I'm not sure Forrest has the experience for this," he told me. "After all, he just got here."

Forrest had only been in-country for less than two months and had just recently lost his FNG status.

"I understand," I said. "I sure wish Riggs, Kelly, and McCall were all still here."

"Yeah, we've had quite a turnover these past few months," Beckman answered. "Everybody's rotating back home at the same time, it seems. I think you, me, the NCOIC, and a couple of the MPs are the only old-timers left."

We set out across the bay headed towards the eastern shore and the headland, which still sheltered us from the effects of the storm. There was a slight chop on the water, but it was bearable. I watched the beach and the mountains of Vung Ro Bay fade out in the distance behind us.

I knew I would never see them again.

We had expected poor sailing, but nothing like the seas that confronted us as the first boat—the plodding LCM—rounded the headland at the far side of the bay, left the sheltered harbor behind, and dove headfirst into the abyss of hell.

Massive swells were rolling down from the north, having their way with the flat-bottomed LCM, which rose the crest of a wave then went crashing down the other side and wallowing in a trough so deep it disappeared completely from the PBRs just a few hundred yards to its stern. The waves were mountainous, sheer walls of ocean water that curled over the LCM's bow and sent tons of water crashing onto its well deck. I had never seen anything like it before. PBR 29 rounded the point soon after that, and Forrest and I watched in horror as *Captain America* struggled up a crest and then slipped into the void on the back side of the wave; the craft engulfed stem to stern in roiling whitecaps. A few minutes later, it reappeared only to go through the same agonizing up and down violent tango, wildly surging torrents of water threatening to overwhelm the small craft with each wave.

"Oh, man," yelled Forrest. "This is unbelievable!"

"PBR 29, PBR 29, this is Three-two, over. Come in, Lee!"

No response. Again, I yelled, "29—29, this is Three-two, over!"

The radio crackled with nothing but static as the boat dove into a valley of ocean.

Then it was our turn. We rode up a steep crest, with maybe just a little too much headway on, and when we reached the top, the boat seemed to stop in mid-air, hanging there before dropping down violently into a trough. The hard landing shook everything, the boat shuddering and emanating strange sounds, cracking and snapping, a deafening noise that made us want to cover our ears in terror. I was surprised that the fiberglass hull didn't break into a thousand pieces. I felt like I was riding a roller coaster, not able at first to identify the exhilaration I felt as joy or fear, until I quickly came to my senses.

It was fear.

I made a quick assessment of the situation. Water was everywhere, and it looked like we were the only ones left on earth. There was nothing anywhere around, not a bird overhead, and probably not a fish in the sea.

We were alone. Forrest and I looked at each other, sheer terror reflected in our faces. The loud and turbulent blue-green seas rumbling with angry foam, the crashing of each wave, was enough to drive a man crazy. Suddenly, Forrest fell against the engine room hatch and went sliding across the top of it.

Just at that very exact moment, I reached out and grabbed Forrest's pant leg. I dragged him back to the bridge enclosure.

"John! You alright?"

A feeble smile spread across his face. "I guess so."

The only thing separating him from the sea had been a small aluminum combing along the side of the engine room hatch, not six inches high.

"I coulda gone overboard!"

"Yeah, I know. Find something to hold onto."

My hands were clenched in a death-grip around the steering wheel; my feet spread wide apart to absorb the violent shock as the tempest swallowed up the small craft. Maintaining balance and footing on the wet pitching deck was nearly impossible, and our muscles were already beginning to ache and burn. We were keenly aware that at any moment, we might be thrown overboard into the wild raging sea. At the helm, I struggled desperately to keep the boat headed into the seas. Forrest and I stared in awe and fear as the seas around us seemed to get bigger and bigger with each passing moment.

Up and over, we went again, flying off one wave and crashing into another. It was a terrifying sight. Down in the trough of the sea, all we could see were towering waves of tumultuous water on all sides. Then, atop a crest, it was more raging wind-whipped foam and breakers with, above, a fine, white mist carried aloft by the winds to cover the ocean like a low, thick cloud.

"Damn!" yelled Forrest. "Are we going to go down?"

"God, John. You sound just like Riggs! Hang on. Get the life jackets for me, will you?"

"I don't know if I can get down below or not," he replied. "I'll give it a shot."

The boat rode up another steep crest, and I looked away for a moment, checking the engine gauges. I turned back to look at Forrest, and he was gone.

Damn! Where was Forrest?

In an instant, my mind presented two immediate choices, neither favorable. Had Forrest been blown off the stern, I might be able to shift into neutral and drift back to him, maybe drifting over him and killing him in the process. I could also try to turn around and pick him up, which, in the current sea state, could get us both killed. I hoped he had gone below and not overboard. I spun around and looked behind me, over the stern. Nothing—or rather no one—was visible.

"John! John—John!"

Preoccupied with worry about Forrest, I was having a challenging time at the controls. The little boat would ride up on a crest, then come surfing down the other side. When it reached the bottom, the nose would dive under the ocean for an instant, sending waves of water cascading across the bow. Each time I was afraid it would continue to go under—down, down, down.

Down to the bottom of the sea.

"Are you calling me?" It was Forrest.

"Yeah," I yelled. "Where've you been?"

"Right here," he answered. "Crouched down behind the #3 bulkhead. This wind and rain is hell on my face!" He popped his head up over the coxswain's bulkhead, holding two faded orange life jackets.

"These don't look all that great," he yelled.

I was so relieved to see him. "Well, they're better than nothing. It's all we've got. I thought you were dead."

Forrest laughed, "Not yet, Three-two, not yet."

Up and over another crest we went. My stomach went also. Seasickness came without mercy—and it visited everyone.

"John! Your turn at the wheel," I shouted, making a beeline for the starboard gunwale to empty my stomach into the ocean.

As the sickness overwhelmed us, we took turns at the helm. It took every bit of our strength to stand at the helm for any length of time, so we made sure that neither of us had to do more than an hour at a time.

After several hours, I reached a point where I wondered what would kill us, the storm or the dreadful retching. And we weren't alone. We would often witness Beckman and the MP hanging their heads over the side on the boat ahead of us, wishing it was all over.

At one point, a piece of grey canvas flew past. "What the hell was that?" Forrest asked. He squinted out towards the bow, the unyielding sea spray half-blinding his vision. The twin .50-cals were in plain sight. "It's the gun cover. It's gone!"

It was impossible to raise our heads much above the coxswain's flat. Even trying to shield our eyes, the horizontal wind sent blinding needles of biting spray into our faces, and the air seemed to be nothing but salt, making it difficult to breathe. Talking to Forrest was an exercise in futility as the force of the wind rushing through the cockpit snatched my words away and carried them out to sea.

The boat dove into a trough again. Tons of water crashed over the bow and splashed into the now open gun tub. We went up a swell and back down again, and again, and again, each time water poured into the gun tub.

Forrest was crouching behind the wheel, trying to get a glimpse out front. "Three-two. Where are you?"

"Throwing up over the port side, behind you."

"You know," he yelled, "We've got a huge hole up front—the damn gun tub! I've got to get the bilge pumps going. There's a lot of water going into the bow. These boats aren't made for this."

"I'm going forward to have a look," I shouted and disappeared down the companionway to the radio room. I emerged just a few seconds later.

"Damn! It's not good at all. There's water everywhere down there."

"Can you take the wheel while I get the pump going?" yelled Forrest.

I squeezed by him into the coxswain's flat and grabbed the wheel, my feet sliding out from under me on the wet deck.

"We've got to get the pumps going," said Forrest as he struggled to get the deck hatch open.

"Three-two! Hold this hatch up for me," he yelled. I left the wheel just long enough for him to reach down into the engine compartment and get the three-way bilge selector valve positioned to the forward bilge. He turned on the pump, and water shot out of the discharge pipe and into the sea.

Communication with the other two boats was impossible. The wind and waves crashing over our vessels made any attempt at using a radio fruitless. I tried to call the other PBR and LCM several times, but they never heard me. They were much too busy having a challenging voyage of their own.

We were a little more than an hour out of Vung Ro when I noticed the MP on Beckman's boat standing on the stern with Beckman's machete, hacking away at the line to the Boston Whaler, which was under tow. When the boat rose on a wave, I noticed that the Whaler was upside down. It had capsized, and the MP was cutting it loose. There was no way to save it. I just hoped we wouldn't be next.

"How are you doing, John?" I yelled, glancing away from the ravaging sea for just a moment.

"This is crazy! What the hell are we doing?"

"I don't know. I don't know."

"These waves must be twenty or twenty-five feet. Got to be!"

It was the roller coaster from hell.

"I wish things would calm down for a few minutes," I said. "I'd like to write a letter to my mother."

"What?" said Forrest.

"Yeah... I've got a funny feeling that we're all going to die out here."

"We've got to go back. We can't do this!" said Forrest. "Look at the old lighthouse over there. It's been in that same spot for an hour. We're not making much headway."

The abandoned lighthouse (Mui Dien)

I had been watching the lighthouse for quite some time whenever I could see it. A few miles outside Vung Ro Bay, the proud old structure occupied a prominent position on the rocky coastline. It would be visible for a moment only to disappear again as the next wave rose and blotted it from sight.

Forrest was holding onto the aluminum canopy stanchion—not daring to even think about letting go. I looked over at him, standing there.

He looks white as a sheet, I thought.

He must have noticed the stare because he stared right back for a moment and then said, "Damn, Three-two, you're white as a sheet!"

We rode for hours, not making much headway at all. Forrest was at the helm, struggling to maintain control. It was challenging to make any speed in the existing sea conditions. At times Forrest and I could hear the water jets making strange slurping noises—spitting noises. Neither of us had ever heard them before.

"What's that?" Forrest yelled.

I shook my head. I wished Beckman was aboard. He would have an answer, for sure. It was very unusual for him not to have a solution to a boat problem. I frowned, deep in thought.

"It's the Jacuzzi pumps," I finally answered. "These boats are designed for calm water river operations, not deep sea. They're not getting enough water. Notice that the noise only happens at the top of a crest—where the frothy water is. We're sucking air!"

"Are you serious?" Forrest said. "What are we going to do?"

"It's almost impossible to turn around," I said. "Flipping the boat around at the top of a crest would be our only hope—if it works."

I thought some more. "No, that won't work. The jets aren't getting enough water at the top of the crests. The boat might not flip around, and then we'd be broadside in a trough. We'd probably flip over."

"There's nothing we can do then, Three-two. We've got to keep heading into the seas. We've got to keep heading due north."

I fell quiet for a moment, in deep reflection. "Damn, I sure hope we don't die out here."

"I don't know. I hope not," Forrest answered, becoming very aware that we were, without question, face to face with imminent death. And yet, amid the towering seas and raging wind, he must have felt a strange calm come over him and managed to give me a weak smile.

The angry, violent sea kept battering us. It was relentless, non-stop, never-ending. Our muscles ached, our stomachs hurt, we were nauseous, hungry, and tired.

We were scared.

We had been fighting our way up the coast for the better part of the day when the boat's radio crackled. It was the warrant officer aboard the LCM, and he was shouting something. We could only understand a small portion of the transmission.

"What did he say?" Forest asked.

"Something about a cove, I think. Well, just follow them, and I guess we'll find out sooner or later."

The LCM rode up and over each large swell, disappearing into the trough as they went. *Captain America* went next—up, up... over, and down. I didn't know if they had received the radio transmission or not. It didn't matter, anyway, as we just followed the LCM wherever they went.

An hour later, I noticed the LCM veering course to port a bit, taking the seas on their starboard bow. "He's going somewhere! Hand me the binoculars."

What a fiasco that was. The only window available for peering through the binoculars was a split-second period at the top of each swell, just before we came crashing down into the trough. I had a difficult time getting the glasses adjusted.

"I thought I saw a break in the mountain range up ahead." I threw the binoculars down next to the radar unit. "Can't see much with these damn things."

As we got closer to the shore, a small cove appeared out of nowhere. It still took us a while to make our way through the mountainous seas to the shelter of the small bay.

The LCM entered first, running very slow and with great caution. None of us had any idea how deep the water was, nor did we know if there was any enemy in the area. They could have been watching from shore, rifles at the ready, for all we knew.

The radio sprang to life. "Looks pretty good, guys. We've got twelve feet of water. Come on in!"

Captain America was next, with Beckman motoring into the calm waters of the sheltered cove. I followed them in with my boat. It was a small cove, maybe a half-mile across. Small hills covered with undergrowth surrounded the bay. There was no sign of life. The boat was calm after having been buffeted and beaten about so for so many hours. It was odd to have it handling in a normal fashion again. All systems appeared to be in working order and intact.

I took a moment to look around. The tranquil scenery was so welcoming. At that moment, I understood how nomads in the desert felt when they stumbled upon an oasis. I felt safe. I wanted to remain in the little cove forever. It was a pleasant sanctuary after the longest, most miserable day of my life.

The LCM had dropped an anchor and directed us to moor alongside. One boat tied up to either side of the landing craft. We ran a hose out from the LCM and refueled the PBRs once more.

"How much further?" I yelled to the warrant officer.

"Not sure. From the charts, it looks like we're just about halfway to Qui Nhon."

"This is taking forever," I yelled back.

"Yeah, but at least we're still alive!"

The group gathered in the LCM's hootch to recover. A couple were resting crouched over on the deck, just outside the hootch door. Every man was sick. Every one of us looked weak and frail, ready to collapse. The calm water of the cove was a welcome relief.

"We should all try and get some rest," the warrant officer said. "We'll have another rough day tomorrow."

The bow was the most comfortable spot on the PBR. Using the life jackets as pillows, Beckman and I stretched out on either side of the .50 caliber gun tub. He decided to join us since his MP deckhand was on the LCM. Forrest claimed the starboard engine hatch. We were just about to doze off when I heard the sound of helicopters far off in the distance, out in the South China Sea.

"I wonder where the hell those guys are going?" I muttered. "There's nothing out there but water."

"Who cares?" grumbled Beckman, too exhausted to speak.

We slept for hours, not bothering to set up a security guard schedule—nobody cared anymore.

We just slept.

The next morning, we woke to a bright orange panorama illuminating the eastern sky as the dawn evolved into a new day. The calm rays of the rising sun fell upon a peaceful and serene lagoon, gentle waves lapped against the shore, and birds chirped happily in the early morning warmth.

We were all starving after throwing up so much. We ate with a vengeance. Food, or rather, C-Rations, had never tasted so good. I was in such a good mood that I even traded my can of spaghetti to one of the LCM crew. I don't remember what I traded it for. The storm had dissipated just as suddenly as it had appeared.

We spent the morning enjoying our newfound shelter. We were in no hurry to go anywhere. Forrest and some of the other guys jumped in the water for a swim. The cove was pristine, quiet, and peaceful.

It felt like we were a million miles away from the war.

While the group was swimming, Beckman decided to take his boat and explore the cove.

"I'm staying on the LCM." I declared.

With Beckman at the helm, two of the LCM crew and the MP deckhand untied the boat and set off slowly, heading in towards the shore.

They didn't get very far.

All of a sudden, I heard the engines roar in reverse. The PBR spun around and motored back to the LCM and tied up alongside.

"What was that all about, Lee?' I yelled from the stern deck of the LCM.

"Big mistake going over there! It got shallow real quick."

Lee opened up the hatch covers for the Jacuzzi pumps, opened the inspection caps, and began pulling out gobs of thick, black mud.

"Damn! This isn't like the sand we get at Vung Ro. This stuff is serious."

We all had our heads glued to the mud fiasco when the sudden distinct *crack!* of an AK-47 demanded our focused concentration.

"Some son-of-a-bitch is shooting at us!" Beckman yelled.

Those still in the water were quick to climb back aboard the boats.

"What the hell?" said Forrest. "I was enjoying that swim."

We finished clearing out the mud from the pumps and fired up the engines. Both PBRs cast off from the LCM, backed away, and spun around in one quick motion. Then the LCM hoisted anchor without haste and got underway. The shooting continued, one round every few minutes.

Forrest ran to the aft .50, chambered a round, and waited, twisting the machine gun from side to side, looking for a target.

"I don't see anybody anywhere!" he yelled.

Someone on the LCM fired off a few rounds in the direction of a small beach at the end of the cove, but it was useless.

Beckman came over the radio. "It must be a lone gunman. Probably some fisherman afraid that we'll steal his catch."

We sadly motored out of our sanctuary and back into hell. The waves were almost as miserable as the day before. We had only been underway for about 20 minutes when my port engine just shut down without any warning at all.

"Damn, John, that's all we need right now!" I yelled.

I managed to radio the LCM, and they instructed me to motor off into a small sheltered area nearby. They arrived a short time later, along with Beckman and the *Captain America*.

"What's the problem?" he yelled across to me.

"Not sure. The engine just shut down. With all that bouncing around we did, we probably stirred up a bunch of crap in the fuel tanks and clogged a filter."

"Damn!" Beckman said. "I think one of the MP's loaded all the spare fuel filters onto the truck. We don't have any extras on board."

"Neither do I," I said. "Anyway, I knew this junker was going to break down. It was just a matter of time."

The LCM backed down close to our bow, and a deckhand threw a monkey fist and line over to Forrest. Attached to that was a 5-inch nylon line.

"It's a real old line," the deckhand yelled. "it's a bit frayed in places, but it's all we've got."

We connected the line to our towing eye located on the bow. The LCM began towing us back out into the rolling seas again. Beckman followed a short distance behind.

Less than thirty minutes later, we went down in a trough as the LCM was riding up another one. The line snapped and went flying across the top of our boat.

"Wow!" exclaimed Forrest. "I'm glad that didn't hit us in the head. It would have killed us instantly."

The LCM slowed, and we gradually got close enough for them to send us a 100' length of steel cable, which Forrest managed to get secured to the towing eye. We got underway again.

We made our way a few more miles up the coast. The seas were still rough, although not quite as severe as the previous day. The waves were still bad enough, though, and all of a sudden, the cable took off into the wind, with our towing eye still attached.

"Damn, Three-two. That cable ripped the towing eye right out of the bow!"

The deckhand on the LCM saw what had occurred, and the landing craft slowed as the crew hauled up the steel cable. They managed to get it over to us again, this time directing us to wrap it around the forward gun tub.

"If it rips that out, we'll be swimming anyway," said Forrest.

This time all seemed to be going according to plan. The cable held in position, and the LCM towed us up the coast. Whenever they would rise up and over a crest, we seemed to be going down one, resulting in jerking the devil out of us. We rode like that for the next eight hours.

We arrived in Qui Nhon late in the afternoon and were met at the sea buoy by a PBR on patrol, its crew offering excited waves. We were escorted into the harbor and were met at the PBR docks by our NCOIC, who had been there all week for meetings with headquarters personnel.

Qui Nhon PBR docks

"Damn! We thought you guys were all lost at sea. We've had search and rescue choppers out scouring the ocean for any sign of you."

"We had to lay up in a small cove about thirty klicks from here, Sarge," Beckman said, leaving out the hours of sleep and the swim.

"Well," he continued, "We're glad you finally made it in. I'm afraid we've got some pretty bad news for you, though."

He went on to tell us that the Viet Cong had attacked the convoy carrying our comrades from Vung Ro Bay to Qui Nhon as they were coming down the mountain on Highway QL-1. There were four casualties.

"They were waiting for the convoy to come down the mountain. They must have been watching everyone pack up the base."

We just stared at him, not believing what we were hearing.

"The guy they called Fat Cook was one of them. He was in a truck near the end of the convoy. They blew the left side of his head off."

The bunker guard who had been badgering me for my Sony stereo wouldn't be needing it after all.

The Kentucky boy—the future star of the circus—future world-famous knife thrower... was one of the others.

Thunk-Thunk-Thunk!

24. Going Home

I was due to rotate back home in three weeks, so I spent the remainder of my Vietnam tour in Qui Nhon. I never went out on any patrols while I was there. With the influx of our crews from Vung Ro, they had more than enough people to operate their boats. I just finished my days wandering around, doing nothing. I remember being happy to be rid of that damn replacement boat, though.

On my last day before departing for Saigon, I went down to the PBR docks and said my goodbyes. Riggs, Rinslow, McCall, and several others had departed months before.

"Well," said Beckman. "I'll never forget that boat trip for the rest of my life, that's for sure."

"Yeah, and I hope we never have to do it again!" added Forrest.

.

Arriving at Cam Ranh Bay for the flight home, I got in line at the airport checkpoint, impatient at having to wait for my final processing. After all this time, the day had arrived. I was going home.

"Next!"

I hoisted my duffel bag up on the counter for inspection. One of the MPs on my boat had suggested placing an 18th MP Brigade armband on top of my clothes, which I did.

The MPs on duty were, of course, all 18th MP Brigade. The MP inspecting the baggage opened my duffel; saw the armband and the mystery girl's photo next to it. I had grabbed her out of my locker as I was finishing up my

296

packing. I decided to take her home with me. It just didn't seem right to leave her behind so far from home... all alone.

The MP pointed to the photo. "That your girl?"

I looked away for a moment, too embarrassed to admit that I had no idea who she was.

"No," I replied. "Just a friend."

The MP smiled and closed the bag back up. "Have a safe trip home."

I was standing around in the terminal waiting with a couple hundred other anxious soldiers. We were all watching a group that had just arrived on an incoming flight. Fresh new uniforms. Fresh new FNG's.

I remembered when that was me. It felt so long ago...

All of a sudden, I heard someone behind me say, "Hey! How have you been?"

I turned around and was greeted by the smiling face of none other than Jesse Griggs, the crying kid from the plane on the flight over, now an E-4 and proudly wearing a bright blue Infantry lanyard suspended from his right shoulder.

"Wow, so good to see you again. It's been a long time. I still remember the flight over here like it was yesterday. First time flying!" I said.

Shaking his hand, I couldn't help but notice one of the Army's most prized awards, a Combat Infantryman Badge, above his left pocket. Below that, a Purple Heart and a Bronze Star ribbon were pinned to his chest.

We chatted briefly and then had to go our separate ways as a loudspeaker announced boarding call.

I thought of how proud his parents were going to be when he returned home. They had sent a scared, sniveling boy off to war. They were getting a brave young warrior in return.

■

Departing the wooden terminal building, I walked out onto the tarmac and climbed the roll-away steps leading up to the plane. Entering the doorway, I was greeted by a smiling flight attendant and the captain himself, all decked out in a snappy blue blazer with four silver stripes on his epaulets.

"Welcome aboard, young fella. We're so glad you survived your tour. Get yourself a seat. I'll have you home in no time."

"Thanks, Captain."

I found a window seat midway down the plane, right over the left wing.

Jesse Griggs was seated two rows ahead of me. He had waved to me on my way by his seat. As the plane started to taxi, he raised out of his seat, turned around, and said, "Y'know, this is only my second time on a plane."

I smiled. "Yes, I know."

The atmosphere on this flight was totally different than on the flight over. There were more than 200 GIs on the plane, very few of them seated. It was a party. They all thought they had won the lottery, which—in a way—I guess they did.

"Gentlemen! Please take your seats and fasten your seatbelts for takeoff," the flight attendant asked over the PA system.

No one heard her. The interior of the jet was nothing but a big celebration. Soldiers were talking, yelling, running up and down the aisle, standing in their seats, or singing. I thought I saw a few with tears in their eyes. It was sheer mayhem.

Sitting in my seat, seatbelt fastened, I just had to grin.

"Gentlemen! Please, please, sit down," another flight attendant demanded.

The big 707 jet roared down the runway and lifted off. The flight attendants had given up. Some of those not seated fell to the floor, laughing hysterically.

I was elated at the prospect of going home after a very long year but at the same time found myself a bit disheartened. I had grown very fond of the Vietnamese countryside, the fertile swamp-like rice paddies, the lush green mountains, the tranquil mirror-like lake that greeted me every time I came down the Vung Ro Mountain switchbacks. I had become enamored with the quaint little villages bustling with people in conical straw hats.

I would miss my comrades of the 458th Sea Tigers who, over the course of the past year, had become like brothers to me. I knew that while the camaraderie among soldiers in Vietnam was extraordinary, it would end abruptly once one returned home. Old friends would be quickly forgotten as new acquaintances were made and veterans went on with their lives.

Staring out my window at the tarmac, I thought of all the good friends I had made: Riggs, the consummate daredevil who never failed to generate excitement and danger in everything he did; McCall and his handlebar mustache. I laughed as I remembered what Kelly had told me one night: "The MPs try not to get on McCall's boat unless they have to. He's too much of a hero and ventures too close to the enemy at night, even turning on the spotlight so he can see, but also allowing the enemy to mark our position."

I would never again have the pleasure of the company of the quiet but steady kid from Pomeroy, Ohio, Johnny Dees—the inventor of the Pink Outhouse.

Then there was Beckman, our defacto NCOIC, always calm, cool, and collected. Somehow, he managed to keep us all focused and out of too much trouble. Thank goodness at least *he* had some common sense.

I would miss my little hootch girl, Missy Soong, who had done my laundry, shined my boots and cleaned my room every day for the past year. I hoped the $5 a week I paid her had been enough. I never did ask.

And old Papa-San. I will miss him the most, I think. I wondered how many times he had flipped me the finger over the past twelve months. Riggs had told him it was a greeting, and we all thought it so amusing that no one ever told him differently.

As the plane gained altitude, I stared out of my window, a lump in my throat, and took a last look at this magnificent ancient country that I knew I would never see again.

I sat back in my seat, smiled, and closed my eyes. I was going home.

My war was over.

LEST WE FORGET

"IN LASTING MEMORY OF THOSE WHO
GAVE THEIR LIVES IN DEFENSE OF THE
FREE WORLD PRINCIPLES OF DEMOCRACY
THAT OTHERS MAY LIVE"

A Memorial at Vung Ro Bay honoring four U.S. Navy personnel killed by the Viet Cong.

LT JG William Turnley Morris III
ETR 2 Norman L. McKenney
RD 2 Anthony B. Brown
RD 2 Thomas J. Meehan

The following US Army personnel were killed during the June 6, 1968 NVA/VC sapper attack on Vung Ro Bay:

SSGT Albert Ishman, Jr.
SP5 Zack W. Napier
SP4 Dennis W. Mourgelas
SGT Angelo C. Santiago
PFC Charles G. Clitty

The four men below were killed during a Viet Cong attack on the Vung Ro convoy during transit to Qui Nhon.

Benigno "Ben" Zamudio
John Conrad
Charles "Shorty" Mitchell
Frank Hiteshue

There was also a heroic bunker guard who was killed in the satchel charge attack on Bunker 11. His name is unknown.

GLOSSARY OF TERMS

AIT – Advanced Individual Training

APC - Armored Personnel Carrier

ARVN – South Vietnamese Army soldier

AWOL – Absent Without Official Leave

BARC - Barge, Amphibious Resupply, Cargo

Charlie – Nickname for the Viet Cong

Chi-Com – Chinese Communist

CID – Criminal Investigation Division (US Army)

CO – Commanding Officer

Concertina Wire – Coiled barbed wire with razor-type ends.

CONEX - Steel storage containers

Deuce and a Half - Military truck capable of carrying 2 ½ tons of cargo

Delong Pier – A pre-fab pier shipped to Vietnam and erected on site.

DEROS – Date of Estimated Return from Overseas

D.I. – Drill Instructor

EM Club – Enlisted Men's Club

FNG – Fucking New Guy

JP4 – Jet fuel

Klick - One kilometer, or .62 miles.

LARC – Lighter, Amphibious Resupply, Cargo

LCM – Landing Craft, Mechanized (54-ton cargo capacity)

LST – Landing Ship, Tank (382-ft. cargo ship)

LCU – Landing Craft, Utility (170-ton cargo capacity)

M16 – The standard-issue weapon for soldiers in Vietnam

MIUWS - Mobile Inshore Undersea Warfare Surveillance

MPC – Military Payment Certificate (used in lieu of dollars)

Monkey Fist - a type of knot tied at the end of a rope to serve as a weight, making it easier to throw,

MOS – Military Occupation Specialty. All Army jobs have their own MOS code.

Newbie – A new arrival

NCO – Non-Commissioned Officer (Sergeant)

NCOIC - Non-Commissioned Officer in Charge

OD - Olive drab

PA&E – Pacific Architects & Engineers, civilian contract firm

PFC – Private First Class

POL – Petroleum, Oil & Lubricants

RPG – Rocket Propelled Grenade

RTO – Radio-Telephone Operator

Sapper – Viet Cong swimmer

SOP - Standard Operating Procedure

The World – Back home, the USA

VC - Viet Cong

REFERENCES:

- 458th Sea Tigers Association Newsletter 'The Riverine Reporter.'
- www.olivedrab.com
- www.wikipedia.com
- Sydenham, Shirley. & Thomas, Ron. 2016. *Vietnam: Animals and Plants* [online] www.kidcyber.com.au
- "The Land I Lost" by Quang Nhuong Huynh
- "The Sorrow of War" by Bao Ninh
- www.crescentwing.com, Donut Dollies in Vietnam
- www.worldhistoryproject.org, Operation Market Time
- "From Blue to Green and Brown" by Lt. Cmdr. Thomas J. Cutler, USN (Ret.)

CONTRIBUTORS:

- Tom Wonsiewicz, former Executive Officer, 458th
- Lou Baumann, former Maintenance NCO, 458th
- Chaz Rynberg, former MP, 127th MP Co.

PHOTO CREDITS

All photos are the property of the author unless noted below:

- Cover photo: PBR 721, Owned and operated by Dennis Ambruso, Elizabeth City, NC
- Map of Vietnam, page iv: Naval History & Heritage Command
- Worldhistoryproject.org, pages 1, 2
- Lou Baumann: forward, page 235
- Chaz Rynberg: pages 43, 45, 50, 62, 63, 88, 103, 140, 180, 201, 202, 211, 213, 251, 279
- Tom Wonsiewicz, LT. 458th Trans. Co. Vietnam: pages 26, 33, 55, 138
- Tom Farrell: page 49
- Warboats.org: Page 79
- David Rosera, 362nd Signal Co: page 44
- David Parsley, LT. 605th Trans. Co. Vietnam: pages 28, 29
- SFC Billy D. Lord, 362nd Signal Co: pages 236, 238 top

ABOUT THE AUTHOR

Michael J. Hebert served in Vung Ro Bay, Vietnam, during the Vietnam War. He was the coxswain of the River Patrol Boat (PBR) *Magic Christian*. Mr. Hebert has been involved in the maritime field ever since departing Vietnam, serving four years in the South Pacific aboard an Atomic Energy Commission research ship, then spending the remainder of his career stateside serving aboard dredges, tugboats, crewboats, ferries, and tour boats. He currently resides in Gloucester, Virginia

Made in the USA
Middletown, DE
09 February 2022

60904269R00179